D0948332

THE CREATIVE ELEMENT

The Creative
Element

*A Study of Vision, Despair and Orthodoxy
among some Modern Writers*

by

STEPHEN SPENDER

BOOKS FOR LIBRARIES PRESS

FREEPORT, NEW YORK

PN 771
S 63
1971

809
S746e

INTERNATIONAL STANDARD BOOK NUMBER:
0-8369-5911-6

LIBRARY OF CONGRESS CATALOG CARD NUMBER:
70-164628

PRINTED IN THE UNITED STATES OF AMERICA

TO

ALLEN TATE

CONTENTS

INTRODUCTION

OVER fifteen years ago I wrote a book called *The Destructive Element*. The general thesis of that discussion of Henry James and other writers (some of whom, like Yeats and Auden, are discussed in more detail in this volume) was that modern literature often reveals a consciousness of a destructive principle in modern society, even where this may seem least apparent.

Writing in the 1930's I thought of this destructiveness as social; a kind of political doom overtaking society. I wrote of a 'political-moral' theme in modern literature, and found this in every writer who was at all concerned with the moral decline of modern society.

There was a good deal of confusion in my analysis, although it may have been a significant confusion. Where I went wrong was in thinking that because I saw a political cause where the writers whom I was discussing saw a moral situation, their vision implied a political view. I was right to think that politics, in the deepest sense, is concerned with the moral condition of society, but wrong to think that the artist concerned with this condition need also be concerned with politics, even by implication. The point really is that a moral view of society can be stated without any concern for social action of any kind, whereas directly politics enters in, social action and taking sides are involved.

Thus I was right to point out that Henry James's vision goes deeper into social causes and shows more awareness of the destruction in the heart of the society he is describing than those critics thought who imagined him to be an aesthete and a social snob, only concerned with analysing the sensibilities of individuals frequenting the best society and living in exquisite country houses.

But though James was concerned with social disease, and though his work is immersed in 'the destructive element', I was wrong to think that there is any implication of action or cure or taking sides to save society in his novels.

Thinking as I did that certain modern works stated—whether or not their writers knew it—social decay, I thought that the cure, not only for society but also for art, lay in social change which would remove the causes of the decay. I imagined a continuous line of development between the writer like Conrad who said 'In the destructive element immerse', and the writer like Auden who demanded of society a 'change of heart'. But actually there would only have been such a continuity if the earlier writers had been at all concerned with social action. They were not so concerned. They were writing as individuals about characters who were also individuals, and for whom society was not 'themselves' but something outside, like the raging elements.

Although a consequence of a literature which portrayed the disaster of contemporary civilization and the decay of all its values might be that younger writers decided to write about themes of saving society, there would be as little continuity in such a development as between a painter who painted storms, and some younger painter who, impressed by the older master's realism, decided to paint pictures of lifeboats in a manner which, as he believed, would encourage people to become lifeboatsmen to rescue the shipwrecked.

But in the 1930's this was not clear. It was as though the younger painter, in depicting lifeboats, thought that he was also creating an image of the means which would save the civilization which could allow artists to paint, with detachment, great storms.

So at this time my mind was full of the idea that the greatness of the literature of the late nineteenth and early twentieth centuries was in its immersion in the 'destructive element', which was the political doom of modern society. And beyond the 'destructive element' lay a renewal of creativeness through the writer siding with those forces in society which would save it from destruction.

*   *   *   *

In the present volume I have retraced some of the steps which I took so many years ago. I have done so by trying to consider not the destructive but the creative element in modern literature.

Previously I laid too much stress on the destructive forces found in the novels of Henry James and much modern poetry, and not enough emphasis on the creative energy of the individual who confronted that destruction.

The creative element is the individual vision of the writer who realizes in his work the decline of modern values while isolating his own individual values from the context of society. He never forgets the modern context, in fact he is always stating it, but he does so only to create the more forcibly the visions of his own isolation.

Of course, individual vision, even in writers like Rimbaud or Rilke, has social implications. But if these were followed, they would mean that society copied the vision of the writer, not that the writer took sides in a conflict already existing within society. There were moments when Rimbaud—and even Baudelaire— were excited by politics. Both supported the Commune, for example. But they did so because in a momentary excitement they thought that society was fulfilling their private vision, not because they were submitting their vision to the authority and order and theory of the revolutionary side.

The main impulse of the whole great 'modern movement' has been the individual vision of writers who, out of their intense realization of the destructive element of modern society, have isolated and perfected that vision.

The 'creative element' has been the amazing release of individual vision *without any allegiance to society*, which allowed writers to think that in their art they were exploring primal values of aesthetic experience. It was this faith in the absoluteness of the poetic image—whether in the poem or the novel—which reconciles apparently contradictory positions: say, the conservatism of Henry James with the anarchy of the surrealists; the violence of Rimbaud or Verlaine (in whom the poetic symbol is related immediately to experience), with the ivory towers of the Symbolists; the poetic angel of Rilke with the Byzantium of Yeats, or, for that matter, with the sexual pair in D. H. Lawrence.

What all these have in common is the centre of isolated creative individuality: the idea that the individual in his own solitude, accepting the modern environment as the 'destructive element' in which he is immersed, can create out of that solitude an 'answer'. The 'answer' of each writer is as different from that of other writers as all personal worlds are different: but those differences have in common the absoluteness of the idea of creative individuality.

So perhaps the 'destructive element' was not, as I thought, capitalism, fascism, the political mechanism which produced wars and unemployment. It was simply society itself. Genius had renounced, or moved outside, society, and any acceptance of a social concept which threatened individual isolation was destructive to its unique vision.

All the same, after the Indian summer of the 1920's, the full effect of a situation which had surely profoundly altered already in 1914 began to be felt. The individual was no longer, as it were, in the position of a statue set upon a building which supported him, and yet which, with marvellously human lines, he did not seem part of: a statue who could declaim against the architecture; a statue who, gargoyle-like, could mock and revile the faith which every line of the building seemed to express. The building was visibly shaking. So the connection of the statue with the building had become obvious and undeniable.

Supposing that the statues could really declaim and were poets and novelists, then their tune had to change. They could not pretend to a complete self-sufficiency; they could not deny their dependence on the building. Even their despair (if they despaired) now became a despair which was not just about themselves and their uniqueness and what these symbolized, but despair about the building itself.

Since the statues were more alive than any other part of the building, then some of them would be bound to say that they must step down and help tear down, or support, the dangerous building.

So the writers of the 1930's have significance in being aware of this situation, and in thinking that something must be done about society. To them that 'something' consisted of participating in social measures in order to reconstruct the society which was the pedestal of their writing.

In thinking this, they did not make allowance enough for the completely anti-social role of the modern writers of the late nineteenth and early twentieth centuries, nor for the completely anti-artistic nature of modern societies, whatever their politics. The curious kind of fatigued disillusionment which characterizes all the art in Europe in the 1950's is surely the result of the feeling of artists in every field that their preoccupation with society, and society's preoccupation with them, saps their vision. How this happens is not clear, and yet it is generally felt. The genius who frees us from the strangling embrace of society with individual vision, by defining and analysing this new situation, will perhaps be the great poet or novelist the mid-century is waiting for.

It can be seen now that the political preoccupations of the 1930's writers were part of a wider movement, though on the surface the directions of this movement were often opposed to one another. The general movement—more important than differences of politics and even of belief—was away from the extremes of individual vision towards the generally shared vision of some orthodoxy. The direction might be reactionary or it might be revolutionary, it might be religious or it might be materialist. But its depths were a shift away from personal originality towards the generalized tradition, from isolation within society towards points of view accepted by social groups, if not by the whole society.

The different stages of development of poets like T. S. Eliot and W. H. Auden show great inconsistency with one another. But in each case, when they are related to the writing of the years between 1870 and 1930, they show the remarkable consistency of the whole development, which has been away from individualist vision towards the shared view of a spiritual community.

★   ★   ★   ★

This book is a collection of essays, written about writers who interest me, to illustrate a point of view rather than to state a thesis. The thesis I might have stated would be that the past seventy or eighty years have witnessed three phases of development in literature. First, there is the phase of highly developed individual vision; secondly that of anti-vision and despair; thirdly, that of a return towards the orthodoxy which had been rejected by the writers of the first phase.

I have traced this development in the work of the writers I have arbitrarily chosen. I have not illustrated a thesis with the massive evidence which could be obtained if I had made, say, a study of certain agnostic, personalist, and Catholic writers. Indeed, in so far as I indicate a thesis, it is only to show the kind of book that might be written on the development of modern literature from extreme individualism back to orthodoxy.

One thing I suggest is that the writers who rejected the Churches and society during the last century raised questions about the relationship of spiritual life, not just to some kind of abstract materialist philosophy, but to the material structure of all modern societies. These questions do not seem to me at all to be answered by today's Catholic and Anglican writers. In fact, part of the present enfeeblement of literature is surely that those who embrace an orthodoxy because the position of the isolated visionary heroes of modernist writing is felt to have become impossible, do not at all answer the questions which those writers raised. Perhaps they are right to think that spiritual existence is impossible without a faith; and yet they do not deal with the question raised by the poets who renounced their faith because, in modern conditions, spiritual institutions had become a relic.

Nevertheless, the present tendency to return to orthodoxy seems to me inevitable. I do not attack it. I merely wish to draw attention to some of the questions the new writers of the new orthodoxies do not raise. Indeed—as regards my adumbrated thesis—the purpose of this book is not to make statements, but to raise questions.

For the rest, my sympathies are fairly obvious. The great experimenters in writing at the beginning of this century remain my heroes.

★　　★　　★　　★

The Creative Element is based on a series of lectures which I gave in the New Year of 1953 at Cincinnati University, when I held there the Elliston Chair of Poetry. I wish to record here my gratitude to President Walters and members of his Faculty for the kindness and generosity with which they received me, and for the opportunity they gave me to write this book. I am especially indebted to Dr. William Clark, the head of the English Department, and to Mr. George Ford, who has looked over these chapters while they were being written and made many suggestions. Acknowledgement is due to the members of the Taft Foundation at the University of Cincinnati for permitting me to quote from their collection of D. H. Lawrence MSS.

Outside Cincinnati I am grateful to Mr. Allen Tate, who has advised and encouraged me; and to Miss Vera Van Panhuys who, when I was teaching at Sarah Lawrence College in 1947, made notes about Rilke's *Duino Elegies* which I have made use of here.

THE VISIONARY INDIVIDUALISTS

I

DURING the past hundred years many poets and novelists have attempted to construct a whole view of life upon their own individual vision. I call the vision individual because it has been cut off from orthodoxy, and when these writers have drawn on orthodox symbols and myths it has been to use them in an unorthodox way. Thus Rilke is at pains to point out that the central symbol of his *Duino Elegies*—the angel—has nothing to do with the angels of the Christian religion. James Joyce draws on the whole field of myths of all times and places, in order to create his own mythology. Yeats, in *A Vision*, created a system based on occultism and astrology which not only provided the framework of his later poetry, but also a private system of categories into which he could fit the characters of all men living and dead and all the phases of Western civilization. An occultism constructed on premises surprisingly akin to Yeats' system told Rimbaud that he was a Magus, close to God and able in his poetry to transform existence.

Individualist vision was the result of the writers' rejection of— or rejection by—society and their endeavour to set up values of their own. A separation of the individualist values of the writer from the materialist ones of modern society is already noted in the pages of Baudelaire's *Journal*, written over a hundred years ago . . . The literature of individualist vision is really the writing of prophets in the desert who, having been driven out of society, cultivate their own visions and return to society with them. But this literature is representative of many people besides the writer himself. Other men of taste and sensibility have also felt separated from the values of their time; and the visionary writer expresses their sense of isolation as well as his own. Since society is composed of individuals, theoretically it would be possible for everyone to feel outside the time in which he lives. The idea of society being redeemed by those who felt themselves to be outside it was common to a great many individuals.

The more separate the writer's vision of his world, the more it was expressed in terms of that separateness of his individuality. The deeper, too, the reader must go to enter into this isolated vision. Thus the more whole and explicit the vision of the writer in his work, the greater the demand it made upon the intelligence of the reader to understand the particular method, symbolism, and even the language of the writer.

The literature of the past two generations is littered with master-pieces which can only be entered into by readers acquiring special knowledge of the writers' imaginative worlds.

Someone is said to have protested to James Joyce that it would take him his lifetime to understand *Finnegans Wake*. 'That is the least I expect of my readers,' Joyce is supposed to have replied.

The impenetrability of this literature is one reason why writers may now have to turn back to orthodox views. The reaction today towards a less individualist kind of writing, and the endeavour of writers to relate their experience to more orthodox systems of thought, which are partly just a literary reaction, happens also to coincide with social changes which restrict the free development of individuality today.

All the same, the reasons which drove writers into the deserts of their own vision have not suddenly ceased. Writers went there on account of the decay of values in a materialist society. Society has not suddenly become less materialist, nor has religion suddenly started to influence its values, in a way in which it failed to do in the mid-nineteenth century. As for the *social* arguments which today tell us to abandon our excessive individualism and become responsible members of society, they are ones of political neces-sity. They are a re-statement, in different terms and circumstances, and within the new context of collectivized societies, of the idea of material progress. Progress, which today has a less optimistic air and is known as exigence, is the same materialism which drove the writers and artists of yesterday into spiritual isolation. Ye day was the day of laissez-faire, when self-seeking individ pursuing their own interests, were supposed to distribute material benefits indirectly to all society. Today is the day of centralized bureaucracy, when governmental institutions are supposed to distribute material advantages, more directly perhaps, to all. The aims remain material and the religions which have recently enlisted the support of a great many writers show as little sign of influencing the new kind of materialism as they did the old.

If we accept the proposition that the isolated individualism of the great writers of the past hundred years has become untenable from the point of view of literature itself, we must none the less question the new Catholic and Anglican orthodoxies—and still more the political ones—and ask whether they really answer the protests of a generation of giant individualists who have preceded us against a materialist society: whether the new religious orthodoxy is not an exploration of 'Death's other kingdom' without there being any likelihood of its relating the values of religion to those of contemporary life.

★   ★   ★   ★

We have just emerged from a great period in modern literature; a period of the isolated visions of the poetic imagination. These visions have more in common with Blake's Prophetic Books than with *The Divine Comedy*. They are the visions of writers with specialist or home-made philosophies and their own private interpretations of mythology. Nor are they confined to poets. For one of the features of modern poetic vision is that the creative writer with a large view of life may well use prose as a poetic medium, thinking the novel to be the form in our day which corresponds to the epic. The endlessly repeated variations in D. H. Lawrence's novels on the idea of a new relationship between men and women which could redeem the world by a revolution made for the sake of individual life is as much poetic vision as Rimbaud's *Les Illuminations*.

Poetic consciousness in this century, when it breaks beyond the very definite limits of the lyrical and becomes narrative or didactic, uses prose as much as poetry to express vision. The phrase 'the

poetic novel' or its converse, the 'prose poem', already acknow-
ledges the endeavour of poetry to conquer the territory of prose,
the felt need of prose to evoke the symbolism of poetry. The
writer today lives in a world of prose: a world of weakened traditions, almost devoid of ritual, ceremony, and symbols within life
which play more than an ornamental role in the community. It
is a world where inventions, statistics, information, politics,
advertising, and abstract ways of thinking about them, can hardly
be digested and controlled within the traditional comparatively
simple symbolism of poetry. There is not, within the traffic of
facts, a sufficient quantity of living symbols to resist the flood of
statistics.

Living therefore in an age of prose, prose may indeed be the
medium most suited even to poetic imagination when it deals
with the complexity and abstraction of modern life. Yet unless
prose fiction is to be a mere reflection of prose life—as happens in
the novels of writers like Upton Sinclair and John Dos Passos—
it is also necessary that this prose should be poetic. These are perhaps the underlying considerations—working below the level
where conscious decisions are made—which directed poetic
talents like Henry James, James Joyce, and Virginia Woolf into
the novel. Theirs was prose written for the sake of the poetic
imagination. The ocean on which Conrad's ships sail, the English
country houses which are the caskets holding the egg-shell
sensibilities of Henry James, the landscape which becomes the
language of Earwicker's sleep, assail us through a medium which
has the effect of epic poetry.

What runs through the work of certain modern poets and
novelists with such different and often opposed aims as those of
Henry James, James Joyce, T. S. Eliot, Franz Kafka, Rainer Maria
Rilke, and even the surrealists, is a modern poetic vision individual in each writer. Whether derived from past religious and
traditionalist values or whether anti-religious and anti-traditional,
this becomes so individual in each writer that it can only be
explained in his particular terms. We have to find a key to his
work in the history of his own development.

Dr. Erich Heller in his stimulating essays on German literature
and thought, *The Disinherited Mind*, notes that in the 1820's

Goethe was already conscious of his impulse to 'escape into the sphere of poetry':

> It is this impulse (which Goethe hardly ever allows to get the better of him), this emphasis on the superiority of the inner vision as against a spiritually barren external world, that ever since has dominated European poetry. This trend became more and more conspicuous with time, so that the Romantics whom Goethe rejected seem almost Realists compared with the later excesses of inwardness perpetrated by the Symbolists.

In the modern situation which Goethe already apprehended, it is important to look beyond this distinction between an external world which is 'real' and an inwardness supposedly 'unreal'. One has to ask what, in a world that is 'spiritually barren' can the real attitude of the inner life towards external things be? Significant reality is, surely, a balanced relationship between outer and inner worlds. The inner world of a writer may become incommunicable, but in a time when the external world has become 'spiritually barren' outer reality is only real in the sense of being factual. The result of that excessive outwardness of a 'spiritually barren external world' is the 'excessive inwardness' of poets who prefer losing themselves within themselves to losing themselves outside themselves in external reality.

We may deplore 'excessive inwardness' but we must not dismiss the literature of inner vision as escapism, just because it is not realism. We must ask whether writers, in creating their individual visions, did so to project inwardly their awareness of the external world, or whether they did so to escape from outer events. If they did maintain this awareness, then perhaps within their inner vision there is to be found the clue to new ways of relating inner life to outward reality.

In 1872, several months after Nietzsche (nursing German soldiers behind the lines at Metz) had been brooding over *The Birth of Tragedy*, Rimbaud wrote *Les Illuminations*, a high-water mark of the flooding-in of Inner Vision. Yet *Les Illuminations* can as little be dismissed as 'unreal' as can, say, the painting of Van Gogh. In its depiction of the desolation of the modern city, its prophecy of disaster, and its affirmation of the Spirit, it is real as

Ezekiel is real, and real as *The Birth of Tragedy* is real. Yet it is not at all Realist in the manner of a Zola or a Dos Passos. Hoelderlin, Nietzsche, Rimbaud, Van Gogh were all of them endowed with an excess of inner vision. Yet their names suggest that perhaps the artists of the inner visions become real when, in their lives, they are exposed to the most savage reality of their times. They are real in their art because they did not use the power of inner vision as a means of escaping from the reality of life.

Real, reality, Realism: these words have to be used with the utmost caution. But we can't at all avoid using them, because it is surely true that the values of the visionary writing of the last hundred years will ultimately be judged by the extent to which it is real: that is, to which it contains the felt experience of modern life. Does Joyce show a weaker grasp of reality in *Finnegans Wake* than in *Ulysses*? This is probably today an unanswerable question, but the position of *Finnegans Wake* will ultimately depend on the answer to it.

The balanced relationship of inner with outer world is extremely precarious, but it may be maintained by those whose awareness of the 'spiritual barrenness of the external world' forces them to create their own values within their inner lives. Rimbaud retains a balance between inner and outer even in his most hallucinated writing because—like Van Gogh—the weight of the real accompanied him like an illness. His delirium is that of the boy who froze and starved in the streets of Paris, not that of self-intoxication. But there is a danger with the Symbolists of the superior 'inner vision' becoming a kind of dug-out decked with flowers—or Ivory Tower, as it used to be called—in which the poet hides away from reality. Writers on the Symbolists and Post-Symbolists (C. M. Bowra in *The Heritage of Symbolism* and Edmund Wilson in *Axel's Castle*) note the tendency of a creative impulse which begins with a religious intensity to deteriorate (as it did in the work of the poets of the 'eighties and 'nineties in England) into artificiality.

The modern individualist vision is characterized by its rejection of the orthodox, the operation which the poet has performed upon his imaginative life so as to separate it from materialism. Even when—as in the case of Baudelaire—it may be argued that the poet is orthodox—perhaps the one orthdox person in an un-orthodox society—it should be pointed out that to penetrate into an orthodoxy which no one else can reach is paradoxical. Baude-laire was a Christian by virtue of being a Satanist, spiritual by virtue of regarding himself as qualifying to attain Christian damnation, and a citizen by virtue of despising the bourgeoisie.

In a world spiritually barren the opposite of what the tradi-tional establishments regard to be the correct moral and aesthetic position may turn out as the only spiritually significant one. In the nineteenth century the only entrance to paradise might be through hell, and in the twentieth the writing which seems to the conventional minded to be entirely revolutionary may be that which has the greatest claim to belong to the tradition. The strangest reversals of roles take place: so that T. S. Eliot, who was long thought of as an innovator, has imperceptibly become a con-servative force, and done so without any Wordsworthian renun-ciation of his early principles and without losing the respect of the 'advanced'. Indeed there is something deeply ambiguous about the position of Eliot, who introduced into English poetry the sensibility of French poets like Laforgue who were extremely 'original' talents; but who yet seems always to have had a profound distrust of originality and innovation.

In 'revolutionary traditionalism', and in a concept of originality as that which is most profoundly unoriginal, there is an identifica-tion of opposite views, what W. B. Yeats would have called a meeting of the 'antinomies'. This might be dismissed as the affectation of writers who regard themselves as superior to a public they tend to despise, were it not for an underlying serious-ness which makes it impossible to dismiss it. T. S. Eliot is both an original artist (probably outside the main stream of poetic development in English, because no other writer has been able to model a style effectively on his discoveries), and at the same time within his unique manner he has intensified our understanding of the role of tradition. Rimbaud, who raged against any religion but his own brand of occultism, provided Paul Claudel with proof of the reality of spiritual life which caused Claudel's con-version to catholicism. After reading *Les Illuminations* and *Une Saison en Enfer*, Claudel describes his almost physical impression of a supernatural existence ('l'impression vivante et presque physique du surnaturel'): 'It is Arthur Rimbaud who instructed and constructed me. I owe him all. He did not belong to this world.'*

His poetry did not belong to this world. That is the operative phrase which illuminates the paradox of the meeting of opposite views in much contemporary writing. Rimbaud created in these extraordinary medleys of prose and verse *Les Illuminations* and *Une Saison en Enfer* the vision of a sphere of poetic existence outside contemporary values. Yet it retains the balance between the 'inwardness' of his poetic life and the experience of the external world. The meeting of opposites takes place within this separate sphere of his inner life, disassociated from the values of his time. His real spiritual existence confronts the real materialism of external things.

★   ★   ★   ★

The possibility of a dissociation of inner from outer realities was foreseen by Matthew Arnold, whose critical consciousness was perhaps in advance of his poetic achievement. Arnold looked to poetry to provide a 'substitute for religion', which it could never be, though it could perhaps in its visions concentrate fragments of religion, broken away from the world. Yet Arnold understood the mechanism of modern society which might make poetry break off from religion, and perhaps even religion break away sometimes from religious institutions, floating off in fragments of poetry: 'Our religion has materialized itself in the fact, in the supposed fact; it has attached its emotion to the fact, and now the fact is failing it. But for poetry the idea is everything.'

The antinomies of the visionary writer arise from the separation of the values of his work from those of contemporary society. Already, even in this act of separation, there is contradiction. His anti-social isolation makes him valuable to society: what takes him away gives him back to society, in his work.

The necessity of such isolation is an idea common to writers as different as Baudelaire from Proust, as Henry James from the sur-

* Quoted in Enid Starkie's Biography of Rimbaud, to which I am indebted throughout.

realist André Breton. In his attitude towards his responsibility as an artist Breton is only an extreme instance of the case of Henry James. In the first, rather famous, quotation here is Henry James defending himself against a parody of the writing of his last period in H. G. Wells's novel *Boon*. Wells held that the novel should be utilitarian like architecture, rather than aesthetic like painting.

Henry James:

> I hold that interest may be, *must* be, exquisitely made and created, and that if we don't make it, we who undertake to, nobody and nothing will make it for us.

And in a second letter, returning to the fray:

> It is art that *makes* life, *makes* interest, *makes* importance, for our consideration and application of these things, and I know of no substitute whatever for the force and beauty of its process.

And here is André Breton, in *What is Surrealism?* (translated by David Gascoyne):

> In the domain of poetry, Lautréamont, Rimbaud and Mallarmé were the first to endow the human mind with what it lacked so much: I mean a truly insolent grace, which has enabled the mind, on finding itself withdrawn from all ideals, to begin to occupy itself with its own life. . . . It was they who really caused us to make up our minds to rely for our redemption here below upon ourselves alone, so that we have desperately to pursue their footsteps, animated by their feverish desire for conquest, total conquest, that will never leave us; so that our eyes, our precious eyes, have to reflect that which, while not existing, is as intense as that which does exist and which has once more to consist of visual images, fully compensating us for what we have left behind.

Fundamentally, James and Breton agree on what is essential: each, that his art is the only surviving means of creating significant values. Where they part company, of course, is that for Henry James the operation severing him from the values of society has not been completed. Although he creates these values in his art, he takes them out of life, and then, as it were, makes them anew. It is an isolated re-making rather than an isolated making of everything in complete independence of values outside his writing.

If Breton went no further than to claim that 'our eyes have to reflect that which, while not existing, is yet as intense as that which does exist', he might even have claimed Henry James as one of the band of premature surrealists. For in stories like *The Altar of the Dead*, *The Great Good Place*, and *The Middle Years* the writer is conceived of as one who can renew within his art a religious experience which has been lost in life. But James is a very conscious artist, creating conscious interest and significance out of the material of the unconscious, whereas the surrealists advocate a surrender to the automatism of the unconscious mind.

2

A vision is a panorama of a great extent of life—perhaps of all life—surrounding a central idea or image. Vision has both centre and circumference: its authority lies in the conviction that a central experience implies a circumference of much wider life. The vision may strike from the outside inwards to the centre or from the centre outwards. In either case the inference of the general application of a single particular insight is there.

In *Finnegans Wake* we are more aware of the circumference of the whole of history (and perhaps also of geography and humanity) than of the centre which is Earwicker himself. But in D. H. Lawrence it is the centre, the relationship between two people, which implies the circumference—society which might be saved by the multiplication of such a relationship. In Proust it is the little cake, the madeleine, which is the fusing centre of a whole vision of time redeemed within the sensation of a moment expanding in ever-widening circles.

The focusing point of vision is often to be found in one sentence, one phrase, one image. Thus in Dante, 'In his will is our peace'; in Blake, 'Damn braces, bless relaxes'. And contemporaries abound in such central notes: 'In the destructive element immerse'; 'These fragments have I shored against my ruins'; 'Only connect'. Perhaps in Joyce's last work the key to the vision is the conjunctive 'and', or perhaps still more the idea of conjunction, in a sentence like the following: 'And it's old and old it's sad and old it's sad and weary, I go back to you, my cold father, my cold mad father, my cold mad feary father, till the near sight of the mere size of him, the moyles and moyles of it, moananoaning, makes me seasilt saltsick and I rush, my only, into your arms.'

Modern literature is characterized by this separation of the writer from all contemporary values, this search for a centre which implies a circumference. It is this search which the Victorians, with all their wish to understand contemporary ideas, to enter into current philosophical and theological debates, lack. With all their perceptiveness and their desire to express a *Weltanschauung*, they compromise with their age even when they most disapprove of it.

Among Victorian poets there was probably more serious effort to grapple with the scientific discoveries and the religious disputes of the age than there has been among poets of this century. Yet Tennyson, Browning, Arnold, and the others failed to create an idiom which could express these ideas, and perhaps this failure was ultimately due to their compromising with their time. A true criticism of life could only have resulted from a separation of their values from the Victorian ones. Tennyson embarrasses us when he writes about Evolution and its effect on religious belief, or about Progress, in the idiom of Keats.

Tennyson's spirit of compromise makes him a social prophet rather than a visionary. He is near to being a visionary only when he is at his very gloomiest. There are passages of *In Memoriam* which lead directly to the pessimistic vision of Hardy.

To compare a few lines from *Locksley Hall* with some from *Prometheus Unbound* will illustrate the distinction between social prophecy and what I mean by visionary writing:

> For I dipt into the future, far as human eye could see,
> Saw the Vision of the world and all the wonder that would be;
>
> Saw the heavens filled with commerce, argosies of magic sails,
> Pilots of the purple twilight, dropping down with costly bales;
>
> Heard the heavens filled with shouting, and there rained a ghastly dew,
> From the nations' airy navies grappling in the central blue. . . .

This is remarkable prophecy, by a poet who had thought about the developments implicit in the invention of the steam engine and dirigibles. Yet, as prophecy, it remains bound to the logic of material developments. If airships and bombers had never been invented, it would contain little which did not seem merely wrong; and as it is, one reflects that Tennyson was thinking of a battle of lighter-than-air dirigibles. The 'Federation of the World' which Tennyson anticipates in *Locksley Hall* is still relegated to the future, and his insight is into potential facts rather than into those impalpable truths which seem always to exist somewhere within the creative spirit of mankind. *Locksley Hall* does not provoke in us the reaction: 'This is a vision of human truth which must some day crystallize into the real!' We would admire the prophecy, for what it is worth, still more if Tennyson had foreseen the gasoline engine.

The early Romantics were true visionaries, what Rimbaud called 'voyants'. In the Third Act of *Prometheus Unbound* Shelley prophesies a good many things which have not happened and are not likely to happen. Yet his vision—whether we approve or disapprove of it—still seems true of a conceivable future because it is true of man's feelings about his own nature. Today we are perhaps less likely than at any time since Shelley to believe that man when completely free will be wise and good. Yet Shelley's wrongness (if he is wrong) has qualities that can still trouble the imagination and raise hope. Shelley is preoccupied by a vision of man; not merely man who has shed oppressors, tyrants, and priests and Sir Timothy Shelley, but man who can create a new world after the image of himself without guilt or sense of sin:

> The loathsome mask has fallen, the man remains
> Sceptreless, free, uncircumscribed, but man
> Equal, unclassed, tribeless, and nationless,
> Exempt from awe, worship, degree, the king
> Over himself; just, gentle, wise; but man
> Passionless?—No, yet free from guilt or pain,
> Which were, for his will made or suffered them,
> Nor yet exempt, though ruling them like slaves,
> From chance and death and mutability,
> The clogs of that which else might oversoar
> The loftiest star of unascended heaven,
> Pinnacled dim in the intense inane.

Such a human being has not and may never be realized, yet he remains as it were among man's effective dreams, and his image might in a hundred or five hundred years still inspire peoples to action. He is real in the sense that we recognize in his image some potentiality that we passionately feel.

The distinction between visionary and non-visionary may be more subtly qualified by considering those lines from Matthew Arnold's *Dover Beach* which contain perhaps the profoundest statement in Victorian poetry of the human condition in the nineteenth century (if we leave aside the poems of Gerard Manley Hopkins):

> The sea of faith
> Was once, too, at the full, and round earth's shore
> Lay like the folds of a bright girdle furled;
> But now I only hear
> Its melancholy, long, withdrawing roar,
> Retreating to the breath
> Of the night-wind down the vast edges drear
> And naked shingles of the world.
>
> Ah love, let us be true
> To one another! For the world, which seems
> To lie before us like a land of dreams,
> So various, so beautiful, so new,
> Hath really neither joy, nor love, nor light,
> Nor certitude, nor peace, nor help for pain;
> And we are here as on a darkling plain
> Swept with confused alarms of struggle and flight,
> Where ignorant armies clash by night.

We all too easily recognize the force of this today. Arnold's poem has that intuition of an underlying future within contemporary events which we call prophecy. But it doesn't create those inner values which are yet related to the reality of the external world, that I call the modern vision.

Arnold draws a contrast between two worlds. One, an inner world of joyous anticipation—an image cast by an outer world supposedly various, beautiful, and new: the other, this outer world as it really is, without joy, love, light, certitude, peace, help for pain. The effect of this outer world being the real one is to overshadow and darken and expose as illusion the inner world of dreams. The inner world is only, as it were, the reflected anticipation of this external one, and therefore illusion.

So, the withdrawal of faith having extinguished the brightness of the inner world, all Arnold is left with is another person in his lightless, loveless world. 'Ah love, let us be true / To one another!' This exclamation is the mutual recognition of two people that they have no world. For they have renounced the exterior world which has no sweetness and light, and the inner one is looked on only as an illusion produced by this. So far as two people can be dead within life these two are (and their situation anticipates situations in T. S. Eliot). They are ghosts standing on the shore from which the sea of faith has receded, with their bodies and souls drained of flesh and dream, their reality reduced to a whisper of 'Ah love, let us be true!' and there is no one else who is not conscripted into one or other of the 'ignorant armies'.

We now begin to understand where vision becomes real. It is when the real itself has ceased to appear real, to seem nothing but lovelessness and joylessness casting a shadow of unreality across the world of anticipation. The real in Arnold's poem belies life. Yet the reality we can make for ourselves in art is the result of an inter-relationship between objective and subjective worlds. If the spectacle of the outside world fails to have anything but a negative significance for us, then our inner minds which are filled through our senses with this outsideness either become negative also or we have to create a reality of inwardness to affirm our own existence in the face of the negation of the outer world.

Yet the outside world does not simply consist of the values of contemporary civilization. It also includes the whole universe, the unexplored or uncivilized, or pre-civilized areas of the map, and pasts of many civilizations which are not part of our own Western tradition and our own instinctual bodies and unconscious minds. When Matthew Arnold says that the world is not various nor beautiful nor new, he is obviously making an unobjective statement based on his own subjective view. Yet this view is important to him because it seems to him the only sincere view possible in a cultivated man living in his time. And, as such, *Dover Beach* expresses a general truth about the state of civilized consciousness among Europeans living in the latter half of the nineteenth century. It is the state of mind of men hypnotized by 'the spiritually barren external world'. Yet once the situation has been stated, other men must look elsewhere than through the exhausted channels of surviving tradition to establish their connection with life. Perhaps they should, as I say, create their own inner reality, or perhaps they should look to other traditions, other geographical and historical areas, in order to affirm the truth that the world is beautiful and various and new.

Arnold states a situation where the poet has become a ghost, banished from nature and history. This position, once stated, is seen to be unacceptable, because although it may be thought to be true by very civilized contemporaries like Arnold himself, it is not true of life. Man is forced on to another level of truth, outside society, outside contemporary history, where he rejects the idea that he is a ghost and reasserts the dream that the world is various and beautiful and new, and that it should have certitude and peace and help for pain. For this is the dream of his flesh as well as his spirit, and it finds confirmation in geography as well as history. It is the dream which affirms life, and without such an affirmation life contradicts itself, denying its own existence, and men turn in on themselves, becoming mechanic ghosts moving in a machine-made society.

★   ★   ★   ★

The inner vision which is the answer to *Dover Beach* must inevitably be tragic. For in refusing to accept the external evidence of the decline of civilization the individualist writers invented values of their own to set against the material forces of the age. What they rejected was not just the facts of materialism, but the faith in materialism expressed in the idea of Progress. The idea of Progress is optimistic, and therefore in rejecting Progress literature becomes pessimistic, and beyond pessimism the only possible triumph of the isolated spirit is in tragedy.

It is, indeed, the fatality of democratic industrialized societies to be progressive and optimistic. They cannot be anything else, because to justify the concentration of all the available forces of

the society in the tasks of manufacturing consumer goods, people
have to believe that they are going to benefit increasingly from
this production. Even when things go badly, the faith in Progress
remains; because it is always thought that without such a
concentration on material aims, things would be worse.

The only literature of our time which is not tragic therefore is
that which accepts the idea of Progress. The writers of romantic
comedies are those, like Shaw and Wells, Galsworthy and Ben-
nett, who do not contemplate the defeat of the spirit, because they
think that social revolution, of a communist or socialist kind, will
lead to greater happiness, more education, and therefore a new
civilization of the Common Man. In the nineteen-thirties horror
at fascism and unemployment led some young writers to think
that they must, in their work, form an alliance with the forces
resisting fascism and political reaction. But in doing so they joined
what was inevitably a losing side, and their work was based rather
on a kind of desperate hope than on faith in Progress.

During the war, in France at the time of the Resistance, there
was a flaring up of patriotism which resulted in a literature of hope
even more intense than that of the Spanish Civil War. These ex-
ceptions serve only to show that the modern writer in Europe
generally tends to think of himself as outside society, and of
society itself as entirely materialistic. Society has claims on his
loyalty only when he feels it his duty to support the good it may
accomplish, or when he feels bound to participate in a choice
between greater and less social evil. When he is unable to support
society for these reasons, he tends to drop out of it in his consciousness and to feel himself more a member of some past society,
from which he is cut off by the tide of history, than of this
materialist one. Therefore, like Matthew Arnold, he is aware of
something ghostly about his own existence which, attached to
the past, only haunts the present. The alternative to Arnold's
position (which, although stated in a different idiom, is not far
removed from that of Eliot) is to be an individualist rebel,
tragically upholding his own passionately imagined values
against the destructiveness of the present.

In a totalitarian society—communist or fascist—every artist is
expected to believe in the theme of material progress (which may

be renamed Exigence) and illustrate it in his work. The dictators are aware of the danger of artists not supporting the aims of their organized and directed communities. Failure to illustrate the theme of social optimism in their work means the tendency to create an inner world of vision which rejects these external values. In Russia, shortly after the Second World War, certain poets were rebuked specifically for writing poems which were considered depressing.

★ ★ ★ ★

It is revealing to compare *Dover Beach* with W. B. Yeats's famous poem *The Second Coming*. This has often been discussed, and my excuse for quoting it again is that I do not think that anyone has drawn the parallel of this poem with Arnold's. Yet *The Second Coming* could almost be described as the *Dover Beach* of the twentieth century.

Yeats begins—so to speak—where Arnold leaves off. The 'receding sea of faith' corresponds to the 'blood-dimmed tide' drowning 'the ceremony of innocence', while the 'ignorant armies clashing by night' parallel the 'best' who 'lack all conviction', and those who are 'full of passionate conviction'. I do not mean that Yeats was influenced by Arnold's poem, but he was writing out of a sense of the same situation half a century later.

But for Yeats, unlike Arnold, the answer to this situation is not to withdraw into personal isolation and appeal to the personal values of another who feels as he feels. It is to accept the situation and intensify it to a vision of tragic history in which our age will be superseded by the birth of a new age:

> Surely some revelation is at hand;
> Surely the Second Coming is at hand.
> The Second Coming! Hardly are those words out
> When a vast image out of *Spiritus Mundi*
> Troubles my sight; somewhere in sands of the desert
> A shape with lion body and the head of a man,
> A gaze blank and pitiless as the sun,
> Is moving its slow thighs, while all about it
> Reel shadows of the indignant desert birds.
> The darkness drops again; but now I know

That twenty centuries of stony sleep
Were vexed to nightmare by a rocking cradle,
And what rough beast, its hour come round at last,
Slouches towards Bethlehem to be born?

The difference between Arnold and Yeats is that in Yeats's poem an operation has been performed which separates his inner vision from the contemporary scene where anarchy is 'loosed upon the world'. The situation of the external world of today enters into the vision he has worked out for himself of the whole of history. And according to the system of his book *A Vision*, to which this poem refers, our world is entering that phase of the moon where subjective values are completely blotted out, everyone wants to be like everyone else, and finally there is a complete darkening of human consciousness until a new phase of historic development begins.

Such an end of our civilization had already been envisaged by Baudelaire in the 1850's. Indeed, it reached English and American poetry by way of the French symbolists. We can follow in Baudelaire's *Intimate Journals* the development of an attitude towards his time which was the background to his poetry. Like Arnold he rejects the values of contemporary society and he sees no hope for the future. (I quote from the translation by Christopher Isherwood, published by the Blackmore Press.)

> The world is about to end. Its sole reason for continuance is that it exists. What, under Heaven, has this world henceforth to do? Even supposing that it continued materially to exist would this existence be worthy of the name of the Historical Dictionary? As a new example, as fresh victims of the inexorable moral laws, we shall perish by that which we have believed to be our means of existence. So far will machinery have Americanized us, so far will Progress have atrophied in us all that is spiritual, that no dream of the Utopians, however bloody, sacrilegious or unnatural, will be comparable to the result. I appeal to every thinking man to show me what remains of Life. As for religion, I believe it useless to speak of it or to search for its relics.

The real degradation, though, is not of external civilization but of the man within:

> It is not, however, specifically in political matters that the universal ruin or the universal progress—for the name matters little—will

be manifested. That will appear in the degradation of the human heart. Need I describe how the last vestiges of statesmanship will struggle painfully in the last clutches of universal bestiality, how the governors will be forced—in maintaining themselves and erecting a phantom of order—to resort to measures which would make our men of today shudder, hardened as they are?

The whole passage is interesting in the light of later events. But it is even more valuable as a statement of the relationship of the modern poet to the external modern world. Baudelaire's positive views of what should be the purpose of life—individual life within the social framework—are also developed in the *Intimate Journals*:

> There cannot be any Progress (true progress, that is to say, moral progress) except within the individual himself.

> Theory of the true civilization. It is not to be found in gas or table-turning. It consists in the diminution of the traces of original sin.

> The abolishers of the Soul (the materialists) are necessarily abolishers of Hell.

> I have cultivated my hysteria with delight and horror.

Since Baudelaire's view is essentially Christian (despite the pagan elements in his poetry) why does he reject the Church? He does so because of its failure to interpret Christianity into terms which effectively criticize the values of modern civilization. Within the rituals of the Church man can still lead a moral existence; he can be damned, if not saved. But it is as an institution spiritualizing society that the Church has failed. Are not the politicians, the journalists, the bureaucrats, the society people whom Baudelaire detested all on the side of the Church? And what language does the Church speak which can be translated into terms of this materialistic life, penetrating it, criticizing it, condemning it? Faith can still exist, but it has ceased to act upon society objectively. This is, surely also Matthew Arnold's thought when he complains that the sea of faith is withdrawing. Why should it concern him that faith is not 'at the full'? Does its 'melancholy, long, withdrawing roar' provide him with any excuse for not believing in the truth, any reason for despair? If

there are six Christians crucified by a populace of a million unbelievers, do the corpses of these martyrs prove that faith is a
corpse?

With Matthew Arnold there was a lack of subjective faith, but
all the same the real cause of his discouragement was akin to
Baudelaire's, and the explanation is to be found in the memory of
the martyrs. The city of the unbelievers is in a criticizing and
criticized relationship to the martyrs. They crucify the martyrs
because they fear them. But the modern situation is one in which
the Church does not effectively criticize a materialist civilization;
indeed, in many ways, it is a part of thè general materialism, the
spiritual death. This is what I mean by the difference between
subjective and objective faith. You can—and many people do—
lead spiritual lives within the Church, but the Church has no
influence on the materialist values or lack of values of our society.
It can be said that if there were more churchgoers then, through
them, faith would act objectively upon society. But this is not
necessarily so. It is more probable that it would merely extend the
split between inward and outward life which is so much a feature
of modern society. Inwardly people would have faith, but out-
wardly they would continue to live in a world characterized by
the lack of faith penetrating its tasks and productivity. The modern
tragedy lies in the failure of the sea of faith to flood external
things.

In the objective sense of flooding over society, a spiritual
institution provides symbols which enable us to feel and think
morally about the activities of external life. Thus, in the past,
through the symbolism of the Church, people were able to think
morally about power—the State and the Crown. Over the widest
areas of life this symbolism provided what Yeats, in his private
thinking, called the Mask: the projection of the personal into its
opposite, the objective symbol. It is the failure of institutions of
spiritual life to fulfil this function which has compelled poets to
invent their own systems, which are substitutes for such institutions. The burden of spiritual existence has been thrown on to the
inner poetic vision. The poets have endeavoured within their
poetry to re-invent all values.

Today there is a reaction towards orthodoxy, and the most

vital movement in literature in the West is religious. It is evident that the Christian orthodoxy of Eliot, Auden, Graham Greene, and Evelyn Waugh expresses more coherent and more accessible truths than the magic of Rimbaud and Yeats, the egalitarian socialism of Orwell. All the same, we have to bear in mind the reasons why for nearly a hundred years writers of genius forsook the ordering of their ideas which comes from conformity to institutions and went into deserts of their own isolation. They went there because the orthodoxies failed to answer the question of how man could find significance in a modern world whose science and aims had no relationship to traditional values. They had to invent their own systems in order to discover their own kind of significance. And although the systems they improvised in the process were full of hocus-pocus, more important than the systems was the search, because it kept open the question which they asked. What we have to ask now is whether the new phase of returning to orthodoxy keeps open this question, or whether it simply is not a reaction from the unsatisfactory answers of home-made poetic philosophies and whether orthodoxy can connect us with the externally barren world any more today than it could a hundred years ago.

II

THE NECESSITY OF BEING ABSOLUTELY MODERN

POET, as everyone knows, derives from 'poiein', to make. The poet is a shaper of his poem, but certain poets, of whom Rimbaud is one, remind us that he is also maker in another sense. Through his imaginative powers he stands close to the formative dreams which are behind the appearances of life.

Modern man in the industrial city is like a mouse who has given birth to a litter of mountains, mountains which are not like natural mountains because they don't stay put. They don't become scenery, the background of the human drama. They are mountains, so to speak, which work on their own steam and function according to rules which, although invented by man, soon get beyond the control of their inventors. They are mountains which may fall on us.

All the same, the mountains do come out of the mouse, and ultimately they come out of the shaping material of the imagination. They are there because men invented them, and men invented them because of the role certain individuals played to themselves in their interior lives.

The classic temptation of the modern poet—of which Shelley and Rimbaud are examples—is to think that poetry can assert the shaping and ordering power of the imagination over reality. In moments of intoxication with their own imaginative gifts, poets have even thought that poetry could save civilization— saving it, perhaps, after first of all destroying it. Rimbaud, at times, seems to have thought something very like this, and he had the advantage over Shelley of thinking it could do so by purely poetic means, and not through a misalliance with political thought.

It is easy to see how such a fallacy can arise. Ultimately everything that we call civilization is projected from what I have called the formative imagination. History consists of projections into reality of man's will, for which we have lost the clue of their connection with the inner life. What once were fantasies and dreams of power and creative will have become frozen into systems, fabricated in machinery, constructed as buildings, separated in their being from their becoming.

The task then of poetry—the visionary poets have been tempted to think—is to restore the lost connection between man-made objects and inner life. If the imagination can reconstruct the image, name the impulse from which the object sprang, then poetry will enable man to regain control of circumstances, find his way among the bewildering complexity of cluttered-up symbols which is the contemporary scene, and re-create the world from the beginning, be Alpha and Omega. Traditions, religions, and the values of individual life will be reanimated through poetry, and will reassert their power of the spirit over *things*. The most remote pasts will be brought into contact with the most remote futures. Magic will be unfrozen from the forms in which it went to sleep—like the Sleeping Beauty or Brünnhilde—several centuries ago and regain its powers over behaviour.

When the poets have become Apocalyptic prophets, it is often difficult to tell whether their picture of a life not yet come into being is an attempt to order an inner world of the mind which they are convinced will have to encounter these events, or whether they feel that the poem is a magic incantation which will help bring them to pass. Is Yeats's *Second Coming* a preparation of the inner life for external happenings which Yeats has proven to himself inevitable through his system of the lunar phases, or is the poem itself a mysterious force helping to bring the events about? Sometimes Rilke writes about his angels as though they are forces projected by the poetic imagination which actually influence events. Rimbaud even in *Une Saison en Enfer*, at the time of his greatest self-disillusionment, still felt that he was an agent for transforming the world by the Spirit, into a world of magic and poetry:

> La science, la nouvelle noblesse! Le progrès. Le monde marche! Pourquoi ne tournerait-il pas?
> C'est la vision des nombres. Nous allons à l'*Esprit*.
> C'est très-certain, c'est oracle, ce que je dis. Je comprends et ne sachant m'expliquer sans paroles païennes, je voudrais me taire.

The reaction today towards orthodoxy repudiates such prophetic, world-transforming ambitions for poetry. Poetry, we are told, is an intellectual, unserious game: the feelings and ideas which the poet puts into his poem may be serious, but he is preoccupied at the same time with a different objective. He is simply playing with words and creating the form of something 'rich and strange'. The satisfaction which poetry gives is not, and should not be, of a kind that changes the world.

*   *   *   *

Rimbaud abandoned poetry too early for us to be able to consider his poetry apart from his life, which inevitably takes the form of a kind of lived poem in our minds. This impression is reinforced by the deep interconnectedness between his poetry and his actions, and the sharp division in his personal history between the youthful poet and the gun-runner and trader in Abyssinia.

His early poetry (when it has the impress of his unique first manner) seems hammered out by the immediate action of events upon his sensibility. His famous theory of the 'dérèglement des sens' expresses the idea that a poet should be a kind of membrane of nerves and sensibilities stretched out by his own deliberate action in order that he may be acted *upon*. *Les Illuminations* is, among other things, a programme for saving the world by poetry. And in the end, after *Une Saison en Enfer*, which is an autobiography of poetic action, Rimbaud renounced poetry for realistic action.

All the same, Rimbaud's poetry is not just the poetry thrown off in his youth by a man of action. It is the poetry of one who with devotion of purpose, understanding, intelligence, and pure intensity acted so as to extract the utmost poetry out of himself. When he acted in this way he put poetry before action—absolutely; just as when he went to Abyssinia he renounced poetry for action—absolutely. The personal solution which might have enabled him to enjoy a happier life was a compromise between the man of action and the poet acted upon in him. But compromise was impossible to Rimbaud. His personal tragedy was a tragedy of the will. If he had had less absoluteness of purpose he would have been a successful man of letters, but it is doubtful whether he would have achieved the extraordinary intensity of the work he abandoned so early.

In the second half of 1870 Rimbaud broke away from the apron-strings which still bound him to his mother, Isabelle Rimbaud, the dour, pious, severe, strong-willed grass widow of Charleville whom we know so well from the biographies. Rimbaud ran away to Paris, in the hope that there he might witness the fall of the government of Napoleon III. This escapade was planned in a manner more characteristic of his seventeen years than were the poems he was writing at the same period. He was arrested at the station for having no money with which to pay for his ticket beyond the first station after Charleville. From gaol he wrote a desperate letter to Izambard, the young schoolmaster who, in intoducing him to the works of Rabelais and Victor Hugo, was held by Madame Rimbaud to be responsible for much that happened to her son afterwards. Izambard paid for his release, and Rimbaud returned to Charleville. Ten days later he escaped from home again, this time going on foot to Belgium and arriving finally in Brussels, where he called on a friend of Izambard who handed him over once more to his mother.

The result of the trip to Brussels was a group of poems harshly realistic in imagery in the manner of paintings by Breughel, but with a music which owed much to Baudelaire. These poems have an immediacy which goes back to Villon rather than to any other poet. Poetry seems to tear its way out of Rimbaud, immediately as an expletive, sometimes blasphemous, sometimes detached and observant, sometimes with a lyrical tenderness. In a poem such as *Ma Bohème* we seem with the poet on his wanderings, and we are struck immediately by everything that strikes him:

Je m'en allais, les poings dans mes poches crevées;
Mon paletot aussi devenait idéal;
J'allais sous le ciel, Muse! et j'étais ton féal;
Oh! là là! que d'amours splendides j'ai rêvées!

Mon unique culotte avait un large trou.
—Petit Poucet rêveur, j'égrenais dans ma course
Des rimes. Mon auberge était à la Grande-Ourse.
—Mes étoiles au ciel avaient un doux frou-frou

Et je les écoutais, assis au bord des routes,
Ces bons soirs de septembre où je sentais des gouttes
De rosée à mon front, comme un vin de vigueur;

Où, rimant au milieu des ombres fantastiques,
Comme des lyres, je tirais les élastiques
De mes souliers blessés, un pied près de mon cœur!

Rimbaud had already, at the age of seventeen, to the highest degree the gift of immediacy: of creating in words what seems a gesture reflecting his sensations. The word *élastiques* here suggests a quality of the poem itself, something muscular, springing from nerves and veins into the life of the poem. It is the poetry of a child acted upon by life and able to express himself with the truth of a child. The poem is, as it were, spontaneously intelligent. No process of intellectualization seems to have entered into it.

In February of 1871 Rimbaud sold his watch and entrained once more for Paris, at the time when the city was the centre of resistance against the Germans, under the National Guard. Little is known of this adventure, except that he had no means of supporting himself, and slept at night under bridges, in the extreme winter cold. It is presumably during these two weeks that one night he took refuge in a caserne with some soldiers, one or more of whom appear to have made a sexual assault on him. According to Enid Starkie, this terrible adventure was his first introduction to sexual experience. The result was the most violent, outrageous, and poignant of his early poems, *Le Cœur Volé*. This poem, which consists of three irregular triolets, is composed of three elements of this experience reported with all the force of Rimbaud's immediateness. They are: the expectorating, mocking soldiers; the classical-minded boy who even at the moment of his anguish places the action of the soldiers in a Greek mythology; and the tender, lyrical feeling of the extraordinary child desolated in the midst of horror for the first—but not for the last—time by the immensity of his own innocence:

> Quand ils auront tari leurs chiques,
> Comment agir, ô cœur volé?
> Ce seront des hoquets bachiques
> Quand ils auront tari leurs chiques:
> J'aurai des sursauts stomachiques,
> Moi, si mon cœur est ravalé:
> Quand ils auront tari leur chiques
> Comment agir, ô cœur volé?

The almost grotesque choice of this highly artificial form, the triolet, used with absolutely no artificiality, immensely increases the tension of the poem, and also gives to it a quality foreshadowing much in modern poetry: a savage irony.

Rimbaud sent this poem to his professor and friend Izambard, who responded in the fashion of an intelligent schoolmaster who is not quite intelligent enough. He was deeply shocked, so he pretended not to be shocked. He sent back to his pupil a rather skilful parody of his triolets in order to show that after all this kind of indecency might not be as clever as his pupil thought.

This action had the result of driving Rimbaud away from the one person who was still a link with his home and his school. All the same, he was pretty well educated, as anyone who reads his poems in Latin written when he was at school (and published in the Pleiade edition of his complete works) will see.

There are two clues to Rimbaud's personality which make it easier to understand—even if no one can quite explain—the intense and rapid development of his talent. One is, that to an astonishing degree he knew himself. The quality of immediacy which characterizes his talent arises out of an un-self-deceiving, uninhibited self-awareness. He seems to have understood the significance of his feelings at the very moment of having them. In *Une Saison en Enfer* he is not only able to crystallize the condition

of his own misery in phrases as precise and self-contained as
separate beads of sweat, but he is also able to see himself through
the eyes of Verlaine, and analyse exactly what he meant to, and
how he acted upon, that 'Vierge Folle'—as he called his comrade
in poetry, debauch, and agony.

The other clue to his achievement is the sharp distinction he
made between happiness and unhappiness. Most people look on
unhappiness as fatality, but Rimbaud saw very clearly that the
pursuit of happiness is most people's fate. And he saw too that for
them happiness is a kind of sedative numbing their sensibilities
so that they avoid awareness of pain.

Happiness confines the soul within narrow limits beyond which
it encounters unhappiness. Unhappiness and suffering are states
in which the sensibility is exposed to a reality none would choose
for his physical or spiritual comfort. Suffering means for Rimbaud
the exposure of the subjective self to objective reality which
pounds down on it with all the fires and ice and space and
emptiness of outsideness. His philosophy of suffering is not
miserable, and it has much in common with Yeats's pursuit
throughout life of his 'opposite'.

Yeats finally discomfited himself and became an old man raging
on a storm-blasted heath. But Yeats spent fifty years moving out
of his own village. In two years Rimbaud brought to bear on
himself the greatest possible quantity of external stimuli.

In seeking to expose himself to objective forces, Rimbaud was
both unmoral and unhedonistic. He sought pain and pleasure
equally as afflictions. His theories of poetry derive partly from
his own preoccupation with the active and the acted-upon, partly
from an affirmation of his own experience in occult philosophy.

On 13th May, 1871, Rimbaud wrote Izambard an extremely
disagreeable letter. It is meant to hurt, and it is the exhibitionism
of a boy who has been renounced by—and renounces—all
respectable company, and it is also the unfolding of a new poetic
doctrine:

> So you're a professor again. You owe a duty to society, you've
> told me; you belong to the corps of teachers; you roll along in
> the correct rut.—I also, I follow my principles: cynically, I allow
> myself to be kept; I unearth antique imbeciles from the school;

whatever I can think of that's stupid, filthy, bad, in action and words, I accomplish for them.

There follows the curious, and characteristically revealing, argument that Izambard's having chosen to return to the university 'stable' demonstrates ('proves', indeed) that he believes only in 'subjective poetry'. The logic is a little obscure. The underlying reasoning is that to choose a respectable profession is to choose to be comfortable, and to choose to be comfortable is to choose confinement within the limits of one's subjectivity. But he, Rimbaud explains, is working to be a poet:

> I want to be a poet and I am working in order to make myself a 'voyant' (visionary). You won't understand this at all, and I scarcely know how to explain it to you. It is a question of arriving at the unknown by the deranging of all the senses (le dérèglement de *tous les sens*). The sufferings involved are immense, but it is necessary to be strong, to be born a poet, and I know I am a poet. It isn't my fault. It is false to say: I think (je pense). One ought to say: One thinks me (on me pense). . . .
>
> I is another (Je est un autre). So much the worse for the piece of wood which discovers itself to be a violin.

Two days later (15th May, 1871) he was writing to another friend, Paul Démeny, developing his theories a good deal further, in the fashion of French poetic manifestos. The only true poets are the Greeks, because with them poetry is in harmony with life. All the rest, except for Racine (the pure, the strong, the great), are rhymsters of prose until we come to the Romantics, who are visionaries without knowing it, and, still better, Baudelaire, who is 'the first voyant, king of poets, a true God. All the same he lived in too artistic a milieu; and his form which has been so praised is really a bit wretched. Inventions of the unknown demand new forms.'

The Greeks are the true poets, because 'in Greece, verses and lyres create rhythm for action. After, music and rhyme become games, diversions.'

All this is extremely close to Nietzsche, whose theory of the Dionysian approximates to Rimbaud's 'Je est un autre':

> The artist has already surrendered his subjectivity in the Dionysian process: the picture which now shows to him his oneness with the

heart of the world, is a dream scene, which embodies the primordial contradiction and primordial pain, together with the primordial joy, of appearance. The 'I' of the lyrist sounds therefore from the abyss of being: its 'subjectivity', in the sense of the modern aesthetes, is a fiction. When Archilocus, the first lyrist of the Greeks, makes known both his mad love and his contempt to the daughters of Lycambes, it is not his passion which dances before us in the orgiastic frenzy: we see Dionysus and the Maenads, we see the drunken reveller Archilochus sunk down to sleep—as Euripides depicts it in *The Bacchae*, the sleep on the high Alpine pasture, in the noonday sun:—and now Apollo approaches and touches him with the laurel. The Dionyso-musical enchantment of the sleeper now emits, as it were, picture sparks, lyrical poems, which in their highest development are called tragedies and dramatic dithyrambs.

(*The Birth of Tragedy*, translated by Oscar Levy)

Rimbaud cannot possibly have read Nietzsche, and still less can Nietzsche have heard of Rimbaud. Yet the above passage reads almost like an allegory to illustrate the life of Rimbaud. And there are passages of *Les Illuminations* which seem intimately connected with *Thus Spake Zarathustra*. It is Zarathustra's dancing star:

J'ai tendu des cordes de clocher à clocher; des guirlandes de fenêtre à fenêtre; des chaines d'or d'étoile à étoile, et je danse.

Rimbaud shares with Nietzsche the condemnation of the 'false significance' of the 'I', which, more than anything else, has turned poets into rhymsters. The first task of the poet—Rimbaud says—is to know himself completely: 'He seeks out his soul, he inspects it, he tests it, he learns it. Once he has known it, he has to cultivate it. . . .' And he does so by submitting it to objectivity, by making it monstrous. 'Every form of love, of suffering, of madness . . . Ineffable torture where he has need of all his faith, of all his superhuman strength, where he becomes the great invalid, the great criminal, the great pariah—and the supreme Savant—for he arrives at the Unknown!'

One wonders what Nietzsche, who said that he had seen all his contemporaries—the greatest and the smallest—naked and had found no truly superior being among them, would have said of the sixteen-year-old Rimbaud.

The objective poetry of which the new race of poets would be the interpreters would be nothing less than a universal language of all life speaking to all humanity. The poet

> is charged with humanity, with the animals even . . . if that which he brings back from *down there* has form he will give it form; if it is formless, he will give it formlessness. He must find a language. . . . This (universal) language will be of the soul for the soul, resuming all within itself, perfumes, sounds, colours, thoughts. . . . The poet should define the unknown quantity awaking within the universal soul in his time. He should give more than the formulation of his thought, than the annotation of his march towards progress. Enormity becoming norm, absorbed by all, he should become truly the multiplying agency of progress! This future will be materialist, you know. Always full of Number and Harmony, these poems will be formed to stay. Au fond, it will be a bit like Greek poetry. . . .

He goes on to prophesy the role that woman will have in this literature:

> These poets will exist! When the infinite servitude of woman has been broken . . . she will also become poet. Woman will discover the unknown.

In September 1871 Rimbaud turned up once more in Paris, this time in response to an invitation from Verlaine (Venez, chère grande âme, on vous appelle, on vous attend). The meeting between the two was the catalytic agency designed by fate to cause both their tragedies. A glimpse of the arrival of Rimbaud in the Verlaine household will suffice to indicate the impression Rimbaud made on Paris in the winter of 1871.

Verlaine missed his guest at the station, probably (Miss Starkie suggests) because he could not believe the 'grande âme' could be anyone so incredibly young. Rimbaud tramped all the way to Verlaine's house, no distance to a Bohemian. When Madame Verlaine opened the door to the dirty, weary, and ill-kempt poet, she was distressed. However, nothing was said and the evening meal of the Verlaine family was served. Little is recorded of that first evening except that Rimbaud, looking at Madame Verlaine's little dog which fussed around the room, commented: 'Les chiens sont les libéraux.' At the end of the meal he stuck his legs up on the tablecloth, took out his pipe, and smoked. As Miss Starkie reminds us, this kind of exhibitionism was not as chic in 1871 as it became twenty years later when the sons of the rich took to being Bohemian. The ladies retired to bed rather early. A day or two later, going into Rimbaud's room, they observed small animals crawling on the pillow. Verlaine was summoned. He explained, with a certain malicious glee, that they were lice.

The complicated story of Verlaine's relationship with Rimbaud, which ended with Verlaine serving a prison sentence for attempting to shoot Rimbaud in Belgium, has its place in criminal as well as literary history. It seems unnecessary to go into the question of the nature and the extent of their debauches. All that need be pointed out is that Rimbaud on principle, and Verlaine through lack of principle, were both prepared to go in for any experience which would achieve the 'déréglement des sens'. Verlaine was satyr, and Rimbaud savage. The meeting-place on their life's journey was that point where Rimbaud's wilfulness happened to correspond with the place reached in the downhill direction of Verlaine.

Rimbaud's goings-on have a place in literary history like Baudelaire's opium, because a principle of behaviour is related to his work. Verlaine's are of quite a different order, of weakness rather than will. Verlaine is a great poetic talent who misses being a great poet because of what one can only describe as a mawkish streak in his poetry. This is just as present (and perhaps more distasteful) in his religious as in his very secular poems.

Rimbaud's temptations were those of the mystic. Living in another age, he is the kind of person who would have slept with lepers out of devotion. Indeed his attitude towards Verlaine in *Une Saison en Enfer*—described as the relationship of Vierge Folle with Epoux infernal—is not unlike that of saint to leper. 'S'il était moins sauvage, nous serions sauvés! Mais sa douceur aussi est mortelle.'

To submit himself to everything, to be acted upon by all possible human experiences and by all climates, this was Rimbaud's passion, and to escape from reality in a way which also brought him in touch with the real. Having lost the religion of his mother, he attempted to force his way into a heaven which he had created for himself, and on which he would perhaps model a new world, by means of magic.

The case of Rimbaud is so extreme that we forget at how many points it touches on other cases of the modern individualist visionaries. For example, Rilke, perhaps influenced here by Nietzsche, also believed that 'the poet is charged with all humanity, with the animals even . . .' Rilke, in fact, would have added a good many *things* to the list. Joyce went further than Rimbaud in inventing a new language.

The most interesting parallel, though, is perhaps with Yeats. For Yeats also used magic to gain proofs of the supernatural. Like Yeats, Rimbaud attempted to construct a system based on the Cabbala and occult philosophy. However, the difference of temperament between the two poets is rather striking. Yeats used magic but neither aspired to be a magician nor to direct the magic against himself. He remained a spectator, outside the machinery which he participated in, not acting and not acted upon. His philosophical system described in *A Vision* is a frame of reference, transmitted to him by others (through the mediumship of his wife), and although Yeats made use of it and wrote this book as the witness of his most profound beliefs, all the same he has an impartial air of being hardly responsible for it. Yeats describes in his autobiography how when he was a young man he saw his contemporaries (the poets whom he calls The Tragic Generation) plunge themselves into various excesses, and he realizes the importance of this to their poetry. But he never applied any such stimulus to himself.

So for Yeats magic was the means for constructing an apparatus which had the appearance of being outside himself and therefore an outside, objective system, where his subjectivity could become its opposite. Rimbaud's objectivity was different. It was the objectivity of himself made the object of the objective. His ego was the carbon crushed by the immense weight of external reality to produce the diamond. He was not in the least an egotist. The 'I' in his poetry indeed becomes 'another'. Nevertheless, the 'I' is also on the side of his will which produces this objectivity.

Unlike Yeats, he is at the centre of his own system, creator of it, responsible for it, and active in its hierarchy.

For Yeats, spiritualism put him in touch, as he thought, with the image-making collective unconscious of all civilizations. The teachings of occultists and illuminists, which Rimbaud found in the library at Charleville, put the idea into his mind that the poet is a son of light who can become an independent creator like God. Miss Starkie tells us he had probably read a contemporary work called *Les Clefs des Grands Mystères*, by Levi, in which the author

> calls on the poets of the future to arise and to rewrite the divine comedy, not according to the dreams of man, but according to the laws of science. . . . When the voyant has become translated into light and has placed his own free will into direct communication with the eternal will, he will be able to direct that will like the point of an arrow, and send peace or turmoil into the souls of men. . . . Whatever sins he commits, whatever action he performs, he will be beyond all censure . . .

but, to obtain these results, he must pay the price of immense suffering.

The whole purpose of Rimbaud's existence, during his short poetic career, was to become his own poetry. He willed to condition himself so that his life was simply an instrument upon which the elemental acted, producing from it words of whose meaning he himself was scarcely conscious. He lived out in two years the whole logic of the poet who, being cut off from the values of his society, passes through several stages of development.

In Rimbaud these stages have the clarity of images illustrating the development of some organism, thrown upon a screen.

The first stage is that in which the poet, separated in his beliefs from the world, nevertheless finds enjoyment and satisfaction in his own sensibility, which proves to him that in an unreal world he is real, and also sometimes vouchsafes him visions of a mysterious and beautiful goal which justifies his existence. This is the phase of *Ma Bohème*. The poet tramps alone through the world, poor, ironic, ignored. His awareness of the hole in his trousers, though, is of a different order to the world of respectable values which he has left. It proves to him that he is alive. He has also his solitary visions which are the reward of a life devoted to poetry and sensibility.

This might be called the primal stage of modern minor poetry. The poet is cut off from belief, but he gains self-awareness and what one might call the vision of the void. For in a world of materialist aims and external bareness, emptiness may become authentic and even sacred. Thus Chekov's *Three Sisters* are vouch-safed a vision which we feel to redeem them in some way, not because they get to Moscow, but because they don't get there. If they had got there, we can be sure that they would find it just as boring as the country they left. Not getting there, there is an emptiness in their lives which becomes pure vision. Eliot's *J. Alfred Prufrock*, who has measured out his life with coffee spoons but who sees 'the mermaids singing each to each', is a more sophisticated example of this kind of isolation redeemed by sensibility. His trousers are in better shape. And the solitude of Virginia Woolf's *Mrs. Ramsay and Mrs. Dalloway* fills an awareness of emptiness and distance with vision.

The second stage is reached when the hostile, or ironic, or ambiguous attitude towards others (which is essentially one of superiority) breaks down, and the poet sees that what is involved is not a choice between persons but between worlds. It is not enough to pretend that the insensitive are mechanical puppets, and that to be saved from materialism consists in cultivating one's own sensibility, and having one's secret moments of revelation and insight. If one's contemporaries are dead within life, then awareness is also only awareness of death combined with the capacity to make memories of life seem vivid. One is challenged to create a world of life to measure against a world of things. This is the stage when the isolated visionary must explore all the potentialities of his own separate consciousness. It is the stage of 'Bateau Ivre', in which Rimbaud makes his delirious voyage through the seas and skies and memories of history and inventions of pure imagination which are possible to the isolated sensibility. But the journey ends at a sea where he is perfectly alone with bitterness and death:

Mais vrai, j'ai trop pleuré! Les Aubes sont navrantes.
Toute lune est atroce et tout soleil amer.

It is the cry of Mallarmé: 'J'ai lu tous les livres.' And it is *Le Voyage au Bout de la Nuit* and *The Waste Land* also. And surrealism——

So the second stage leads to the exhaustion of all the possibilities of isolated creativeness, and leaves an emptiness without vision, the death of the self coinciding with the death of society. The only thing is to eliminate the self, and so we come to the third stage, which is that of the projection of systems.

In this third stage the poet realizes that he abandoned religion because it did not provide him with myths and symbols to which he could relate his experience of modern life. Apart from this, and because of it too, he objected to its morality, which, while labelling the defects which are among the few qualities in which modern man remains human, sinful, is ineffective in the world of science and progress. The poet sees now that it is not enough for him to be sensitively aware of this situation. It is not enough even for him to explore all the limits of his isolated consciousness and create a world of fantastic imaginings, pure poetry. He has to go forward and invent a new system which will give meaning to the world. The symbolic language of religion has become frozen within the orthodoxy of the Churches and the institutionalism which is bound up with other institutions and hence with the materialism of the modern world. Yet poetry remains a symbolic language capable of renewing itself, and being applied to new situations in the idioms and forms invented by new poets. All that is required (and it is certainly a tremendous order) is that the poets should become prophets. They must develop the implications of the images and idiom they use to express their personal experiences and discover a philosophy. In order to do this, they must cease to be subjective and become objective. And they must learn about all myths and past religious systems in order to transform them and apply them to the modern situation.

Moreover the poet does not need to do this only on account of the spiritual crisis in the world. He needs to do it also for the sake of his own poetry. Unless there are metaphors which exist outside the poetry and can be referred to, like a dictionary, then the further the poet explores his own consciousness, the more obscure his work will be to the reader, the greater the difficulty of communication.

Hence Yeats's categories in *A Vision* are partly expected to change the world and partly they have the more modest aim 'of providing metaphors for my poetry'.

But to invent a private religious philosophy for the sake of poetry and to compensate for the inadequacy of existing systems is also to expose oneself to the criticism of those more coherent systems. To construct an orthodoxy of one's own is to lead back to a more tested orthodoxy. Rimbaud's magic leads straight into Claudel's catholicism.

Since Rimbaud, with his passion for action, tended to become his poetry in his life, his own existence is the test of his philosophy. It led him from the ecstatic hallucination of *Les Illuminations* to the Hell of *Une Saison en Enfer*.

Here he is being the magic of *Les Illuminations*:

> Il est l'amour, mesure parfaite et réinventée, raison merveilleuse et imprévue, et l'éternité: machine aimée des qualités fatales. Nous avons tous eu l'épouvante de sa concession et de la nôtre: ô jouissance de notre santé, élan de nos facultés, affection égoïste et passion pour lui, lui qui nous aime pour sa vie infinie...
>
> Et nous le rappelons et il voyage... Et si l'Adoration s'en va, sonne, sa promesse sonne: 'Arrière ces superstitions, ces anciens corps, ces ménages et ces âges. C'est cette époque-ci qui a sombré!'

There follows the terrible awakening from the individual vision, in *Une Saison en Enfer*:

> Les hallucinations sont innombrables. C'est bien ce que j'ai toujours eu: plus de foi en l'histoire, l'oubli des principes. Je m'en tairai: poëtes et visionnaires seraient jaloux. Je suis mille fois le plus riche, soyons avare comme la mer.
>
> Ah çà! l'horloge de la vie s'est arrêtée tout à l'heure. Je ne suis plus au monde.—La théologie est sérieuse, l'enfer est certainement *en bas*—et le ciel en haut.—Extase, cauchemar, sommeil dans un nid de flammes.
>
> Que de malices dans l'attention dans la compagne... Satan, Ferdinand, court avec les graines sauvages...Jésus marche sur les ronces purpurines, sans le courber...Jésus marchait sur les eaux irritées. La lanterne nous le montra debout, blanc et des tresses brunes, au flanc d'une vague d'émeraude...

Thus we come to the fourth stage, which is that of return to society and perhaps to some form of orthodoxy. With Rimbaud the return was far from complete. His savage nature could not conform, but his suffering, his intelligence, and his gift bring him, as it were, under the fire of the idea he had forsaken in order to invent his own system. Where he left off, others who were influenced by him, like Claudel and St. Jean Perse, went on.

At the end of *Une Saison en Enfer* Rimbaud seems, indeed, to wish to reconcile Christianity with Saint-Simonist socialism. 'Le combat spirituel est aussi brutal que la bataille d'hommes; mais la vision de la justice est le plaisir de Dieu seul.' But there his work breaks off, and he goes to Abyssinia. It is impossible to interpret him further.

'Il faut être absolument moderne', is another of the observations with which he abandons poetry. It is perhaps a slogan for the life of action which he is now about to embark on; it is also an epitaph on what has gone before. His aim always had been to unite within his own being the supernatural with the most real circumstances of contemporary living.

In one of the few references he ever made later to poetry, he said he had given it up because to continue would have meant to go mad. Given the discipline by which he attained his 'objectivity', there can be little doubt that this was true. There are passages of *Une Saison en Enfer* which seem symptomatic of mental disorder.

His poetic aims have been related to surrealism, but really they are unlike anything else. The surrealists used certain techniques—such as automatic writing—for breaking down the logical connection between thoughts. But Rimbaud was breaking down much more than this. He was attempting to remove the barrier which divides subject from object, the 'I' from the 'not-I', and to make his sensibility an instrument played upon by universal mind.

Today that attempt would probably be condemned, because it was the result of the action of the will, and because it resulted in too much that was confusing. All the same, he cannot just be dismissed as a prodigy. His poetry has certain qualities which no other modern poetry has attained. The most striking of these is the purification (especially in *Les Illuminations*) of his images of everything except what seems some essential irreducible primal quality, hard as a jewel through which there shines a light not of this world. Immediately in the opening lines of *Les Illuminations* we enter this world of hardness, colour, and preternatural light:

> Aussitôt que l'idée du Déluge se fût rassise,
>
> Un lièvre s'arrêta dans les sainfoins et les clochettes mouvantes, et dit sa prière à l'arc-en ciel à travers la toile de l'araignée.

If one deplores his obsessive and very literally carried-out sincerity, thinking that it is better suited to action than to poetry, one should remember also that he failed as a man of action, and that his idea of action was nearer to that of a saint or mystic than of a business man. Also his preoccupation with action did not (as is the case with a poet like Aragon) introduce an impure element into his poetry. On the contrary, it is the idea of action which gives it that strangeness in which one feels the presence of another world. Rimbaud did not think that poetry was a game. He thought it was the expression in rhapsodic words of a reality which had entered completely into the being of the poet, abolishing his ego and making him a vehicle for nothing but itself.

Yeats was a poet who dabbled in the occult. His poems are often concerned with the supernatural, but I do not suppose that any reader has ever for a moment felt the *presence* of the supernatural in a poem of Yeats. In his poetic sincerity Rimbaud was unsurpassed, and today when people talk of poetry as an 'intellectual game', his example exists as a challenge in the most extraordinary spiritual outposts conquered by modern poetry.

III

RILKE AND THE ANGELS,
ELIOT AND THE SHRINES

THE poet as hero! If Carlyle were writing today a twentieth-century *Heroes and Hero-Worship*, he would certainly note that phenomenon of our time, the culture hero, the one who—as E. M. Forster wrote of T. S. Eliot in his early poetry—while other people are talking of war, complains about drawing-rooms, and whose protest is all the more effective because it is faint.

The biographers—and his own letters—establish Rainer Maria Rilke as an example of this kind. While others were engaged in recommending action he, who was brought up in a family with a military tradition and was sent at an early age to a military academy, spent his whole life nursing his poetic talent. When, once or twice, he faltered, he achieved tremendous applause and a success from which it was difficult to withdraw. There was *Cornet Christopher Rilke*, in which he celebrated the loves and adventures of a supposed ancestor in the Thirty Years' War. On this disowned work Rilke's popular success—that 'sum of mis-understanding'—in Germany was based. Then there was the series of War God poems written in the first days of 1914, when so many in so many countries lost their heads. But Rilke soon re-covered, and spent much of the war hidden away—like some character in a story of Kafka who has turned into a parasite—in the Archives Department of the War Office at Vienna, where he spent his time ruling lines on sheets of paper, on which others worked out sums. He wrote almost no poetry throughout the war; only letters, endlessly complaining, protesting, weakly, in-effectively, whispering the secrets of survival: 'You are quite right, whoever now makes himself bigger, freer, and more human in his own existence, is doing his part towards peace—as yet it must be worked at *in an inward direction*, not until a few have it all big and ready within them can it let itself be brought into the world.'*

As a small child, he was brought up by his mother to resemble the girl she wished to have had. He was called Sophie, had long hair and dolls to play with. At the age of eleven his childhood became the object of his father's fantasies. His father was frustrated in his military career, so Rilke was switched from being mother's darling to being father's wish: a cadet at the military academy at St. Poelten. Between 1886 and 1891 he was about as unhappy as an extremely sensitive child can be.

For the rest of his life he was more or less cared for, psychologically as well as materially. His marriage, which put too great strain on his poetic talent, lapsed rather than was dissolved. He was fortunate in finding princesses and countesses with castles and mansions who gave him hospitality. Other human beings—particularly women—he set at a distance in those great involved letters expressing emotional proximity to people, some of whom he would never even see. Letters played much the same role in Rilke's life as the cork lining that shut off the noises of the world from Proust's room. He died of an illness resulting from an infection contracted by the thorn of a rose sticking into a finger. So his life seems enclosed between parentheses of fairy-tale childhood and fairy-tale death.

Some things about Rilke—a certain deeply ingrown affectation and an inability, at times, to distinguish between his own feelings and those of others—are rather tiresome. The tiresomeness comes out particularly in the letters. Nevertheless it remains true that Rilke's life is rightly considered the pattern of the heroic modern artist. One accepts almost without question his defects because his qualities grow out of them. He shows how in an age where heroism almost inevitably seems connected with war and politics, it is still possible to gain a significant victory over oneself.

Rilke, is, in particular, a hero of those who call themselves 'personalists'. It is easy to understand why. Except for the very successful series of poems about the Paris Zoo, and about certain

* Wartime Letters of R. M. Rilke, translated by M. D. Herter Norton.

works of art, Rilke's poems are hardly ever completely separated from Rilke. Often he seems to be *using* poetry as a means towards attaining some personal spiritual end, rather than creating a poem separate from all other poems. In his early work he uses it to prove to himself that the outside world exists, even that he himself exists, and that the gulf between inner and outer worlds can be bridged. There is a lack of a hard clear edge between one poem and another. One may guess that, aware of this defect, at a certain stage of his development, when he was in Paris, he concentrated on subjects outside himself in order to separate each poem from the stream of his poetic thinking, which flows as much through his letters as his poetry.

The need which gave him the tendency to use poetry so subjectively doubtless arose from that period in his childhood when he was effectively (and for life) cut off from being the kind of person who is real to himself and to others, and who finds them real . . . After maturity he reached towards life through his poetry, and through his habit of poeticizing people and experiences in letters, where they acquire a kind of existence only in his terms. Often the process is rather suspect and amounts almost to self-deception, if not hypocrisy. There is a tendency to translate actual events into an almost hallucinatory inner language. One cannot help feeling that Rilke does this because the actual is inaccessible to him unless it flows into his own Rilkean thoughtstream where everything is in the process of liquefying into the subjectively poetic. Here is an extract of an account of an early meeting with Clara Westhoff the sculptress (later to become his wife) and her friend, the painter Paula Becker:

> As I sat there, holding up Clara's great wreath of heather with those brown eyes opposite me, I could feel how the twigs she had forced into a circle radiated the simple and devout strength of her sculptor's hands, and thus the one girl's strength communicated itself to my own raised hands, while the other's dear face gave me a sweetness that was courageous with all its humility. . . .

With Lawrence, such a description would imply a real confrontation with the girls. Whereas with Rilke, we feel it an evasion of the reality. There is confusion between subject and object (himself and the girls themselves) which is quite frequent with him. His own subjective feelings are projected into others without his knowing either himself or them sufficiently for such an identification to be significant. The same doubt arises when he explains his marriage, in another letter: 'the really good marriage is that in which each partner makes the other the guardian of his or her solitude . . .'. Soon after he had written these lines, he left his wife, their daughter having been born. Poverty, the incessant noise of a real baby, and Clara having to get on with her sculpture were too much for solitude. All this is understandable. There is no justification for passing judgement on Rilke for egotism and selfishness. What is revealing is the lack of knowledge of himself, his wife, and babies in the earlier statement. There has been a confusion of poetic thinking with living values, and Rilke's letters provide hundreds of examples of this kind of poeticization of reality.

Rilke's only development was, really, in his poetry. His relations with living were purely diplomatic, poetry being used as an excuse for an avoidance of life. But within the false poetic development of most of the letters, the real poetry also developed: that is what is so wonderful. In his isolation, it became a way of life, even through the years when he would write no poetry.

The problem was, in this isolation, to find his way step by step back to his own reality, from which he had been cut off by childhood. His letters become authentic when he is writing about his own earliest experiences. His mother—he tells a correspondent—was utterly unreal: 'My mother used to pray as other people drink a cup of coffee.' In addition to his being brought up to play the part of little Sophie, his baptismal names, Réné (which later he changed to Rainer) and Maria, were ambiguous, applying equally to boy or girl. His father, Joseph Rilke, who had distinguished himself at the siege of Brescia in the Austrian campaign of 1859 in Italy, and who was invalided out of the army without having acquired the patents of an officer, is described by Rilke as being incapable of love, and having an indescribable fear of every feeling that came from the heart. Above all he showed no tenderness of affection for his son.

In 1920, many years after Rilke had been at St. Poelten, Major-General von Sedlakowitz, Rilke's former German teacher at the academy, wrote to the now famous poet to inquire whether he was indeed the Réné Maria Rilke whom he had taught at the military academy. He got more than he had asked for. Rilke, after waiting for some time spent in choking back his indignation, wrote that he had hesitated to answer the letter at all, because it seemed to him scarcely credible that a voice could come out of such a past. He believed—he went on—that he could hardly have lived his life, if he had not, for several years now, denied and repressed all memory of the five years of military training. 'There have been times when the slightest reminder of that rejected past would have destroyed the new fruitful and individual consciousness which I was striving to attain.' He adds that he only learned later, from reading Dostoyevsky's *The House of the Dead*, that 'there exists, at least in the Slav soul, a degree of submission which may well be called perfect: even weighed down by the most immediate pressure, the soul creates a secret place, a further dimension of existence where true liberty can be found, however painful outward conditions may become'.

Elsewhere he described how he began at St. Poelten to rejoice in his sufferings and to attach a mystical religious significance to them. He even says (there is little humour in Rilke) he had the experience of stigmata appearing on the soles of his feet.*

Suffering and dolls are perhaps the connecting links between Rilke and outside reality. The dolls he played with became symbols for beings who, unlike his mother, looked and acted consistently, and remained true to the emotions and actions he projected into them. Dolls and puppets fill in his work the curious role of intermediaries between a human life which is so discontinuous and unreal as to exist only intermittently, and an ideal existence sustained solidly and continuously. By 'real' he meant a kind of being in which the outer appearance is wholly consistent with the inward thought and feeling. He wanted 'outwardness' to be a gesture perfectly reflecting an inner continuity. The angels of the *Duino Elegies* are exactly this: fusions of inward and outward qualities in which two existences, physical appear-

---

* Most of the information in this chapter is taken from *Rilke, Man and Poet*, by Nora Wydenbruck, a rather humourless biography, but perhaps the most informative. E. M. Butler's biography may also be recommended.

ance and spiritual inwardness, gaze like mirrors into one another, intaking and exhaling light. 'Angel and doll!' he exclaims in the Fourth Elegy:

> Engel und Puppe: dann ist endlich Schauspiel.
> Dann kommt zusammen, was wir immerfort
> entzwein indem wir da sind.

> Angel and doll! Then there's at last a play!
> Then we unite what we continually
> part by our being there.*

Dolls, then, are realer than human beings with their purposelessness, their broken, fragmentary existence.

Possibly there is also a connection between Rilke's idea of puppets and his attitude towards works of art. Into paintings and sculpture men have projected a purposiveness, a consistency of mood, which is not in themselves. Art is the proof of objective being, the assertion of existence. In his letters to his wife about his discovery of Cézanne, he always emphasizes objectivity and existence. And in a curious letter in which he links up Cézanne's painting with Baudelaire's poem *Charogne*, one sees that what he admires in the French poet and the French painter is that both discovered and asserted existence in unlikely places: '. . . The artist's vision had so far to conquer itself that it could see in everything terrible or seemingly merely repugnant the existing which is valid like everything that exists. The creative artist is not permitted to select or to turn away from any form of existence. . . .' He was painfully occupied in using poetry to prove to himself that other things exist, that he existed. He had to translate these things into terms of an idea which he had formed for himself of what existence should be. He wanted life like angels, like dolls, like the Archaic statue of the early Apollo staring at you with eyes all over his body, life whose significance is crystalline, concrete and also symbolic, for ever breaking beyond the limits of flesh and consciousness into an indestructible continuity. Thus lovers: lovers were surely seeking for something in one another which

---

* *Duino Elegies*—the translation by J. B. Leishman and Stephen Spender is used throughout this chapter.

was not precipices, gulfs, abysms of emptiness, discontinuity. Perhaps, though, the lover only achieves the fullest realization of such a continuity of feeling when love is unrequited. And heroes: heroes were surely breaking beyond themselves into an action where life became symbol, so that in death they attained the fulfilment of their purpose. And saints . . .

Beyond these examples, though, there lie two continuities: the womb and death. These are the boundaries of Rilke's world, at the one extreme the womb, the world of the 'nowhere-without-no', where existence is one with what it exists upon, giving is receiving, and everything its own opposite. At the other extreme is death, the death which is the fulfilment of the whole of a life-time, like the fruit of the blossom. But beyond death, he cannot surrender existence to God. God exists in him and without him God could not exist. 'Was wirst du tun, Gott, wenn ich sterbe?' he cries. 'God, how will you exist without me?' His God 'is life and death as a whole, he is all Being, he is both the Creator and the created, both father and son'.*

Between these extremes of death and womb, he pieced his own existence together, as it were, out of fragments of his own reality which he found lying about Europe, on journeys, in museums and art galleries, sometimes in books, and occasionally in the glance of eyes or in a figure standing at the end of a street, a beggar on a bridge. He went to Russia, to France, to Italy, to Spain: but everywhere he contained within himself the shuttered atmosphere of an attic in which he pieced together the fragments of a vase.

His great discovery was that in taking these fragments of a great outsideness into his work and making them himself, he also gave them back to themselves. He gave the things which he loved and lingered over and named a new and unique existence. And within himself he ultimately created a world:

> Sind wir vielleicht *hier*, um zu sagen: Haus,
> Brücke, Brunnen, Tor, Krug, Obstbaum, Fenster,—
> Höchstens: Säule, Turm. . . . aber zu sagen verstehs,
> oh zu sagen *so*, wie selber die Dinger niemals innig
> meinten zu sein. . . .

* Quotation from notes of Vera Van Panhuys.

> Are we, perhaps, here just for saying: House,
> Bridge, Fountain, Gate, Jug, Olive-tree, Window,—
> possibly: Pillar, Tower? . . . . but for saying, remember,
> oh for such saying as never the things themselves hoped
> so intensely to be. . . .

At first he learned the art of putting together outer and inner worlds from artists who did it most demonstrably: painters and sculptors whose manner of working interested him more perhaps than did their work. As he wrote to the painter Otto Modersohn of the artists' colony at Worpswede to which he himself had belonged for a time, 'the path through your work led me at many places nearer to myself, much became clear to me through it, much is thereby linked together for me forever . . .'. His wife was a sculptress, and when their ménage broke up he became secretary to Rodin. Sculpture was perhaps more of a lesson to him than painting. He learned from it that he must not only make the Pictures in Words of his early poetry, but that he must shape his poems.

Just as Van Gogh's painting is different from that of the other Post-Impressionists, so Rilke's poetry is different from that of other poets like Stefan George and von Hofmannsthal who were his contemporaries, and who may at a first glance seem to have similar aims. The difference is that every poem is like a drop of blood coming from the same life rather than an artefact bearing the imprint of the same hand. Everything comes from an interior life where even the most outside things—which both Van Gogh and Rilke ardently pursue—are given this interior quality. Viewed as a whole, the development of the work is an ascent of steps climbing to some goal which perhaps lies outside the art at the point where the artist discovers the 'truth' which makes further expression unnecessary. The poetic system attains its completest summation and statement in the *Duino Elegies*. Rilke announces in July 1922 to his publisher, Kippenberg, that his *Collected Poems* are now complete, 'in every sense of the word'. Three years later, in 1926, he dies.

The difference between Van Gogh and the other Post-Impressionists might be that *they* painted out of their existences, whereas *he* existed out of his painting. So, too, Rilke existed through his poetry, and when the poetry had achieved the purpose of, as it were, completing the round of his existence, he was finished. However much the subjective approach may achieve by absorbing impressions from the outside and converting them into invisible interior world, ultimately it reaches limits of absorption. The subjective harmony is as complete as it can ever be, for its potentialities are limited by the artist's own limitations and not by inexhaustible nature or objective faith—the accumulation of generations—into which he can enter. A poet like Eliot sheds the subjective element in himself as he develops. His growth consists in entering what is outside and impersonal, an ever-extending objectivity.

Van Gogh, like Rilke, at times took other works of art as the subjects of his painting: Millet, Delacroix, and even Japanese paintings. Rilke made translations of sonnets by Michelangelo, Louise Labbé, and Elizabeth Barrett Browning. Perhaps both artists did this because they wished to enter into the objective method of another artist and to transfer this objectivity into their own subjective art. They did it to gain strength from a new and different approach. A work of art by an artist with an objective attitude was to them a bridge with the outside world.

Rilke creates such a bridge in the beautiful and famous sonnet on the Archaic statue of the Apollo. The torso of the Apollo glows like a candelabrum with the gaze which is absent from the missing head. The sonnet goes on to describe this gaze, distributed all over the Apollo's body, looking back at the beholder:

> denn da ist keine Stelle,
> die dich nicht sieht. Du musst dein Leben ändern.

> For there is no place here that does not see you.
> You must change your life.

The statue first serves as an outside object, an art-work, through whose example Rilke is able to create his independent-looking poetic form, establishing connection with the being outside his own existence. But he then turns it into a peculiarly Rilkean symbol, an inside object. The spectator looking at the statue and the statue looking at the spectator become existences mirroring one another of a kind which foreshadows the angel in whose shape there is the perfect equilibrium of inner and outer worlds.

The last words of the sonnet are extraordinarily abrupt: 'Du musst dein Leben ändern.' In them, the poetry steps as it were out of the particular poem and moves into the main stream of all Rilke's poetry. From the statue, Rilke takes into his poetry the lesson that art is the transformation of his life through his poetry.

Rilke strove through poetry to attain what he had called in the letter to Major-General von Sedlakovitz 'the new fruitful individual consciousness'. He pieced the wholeness of himself together from fragments of outside life corresponding to gaps in his own consciousness. But all the time he was growing ever more aware that in taking these things into himself he was also giving them a new existence, performing a task of transformation, creating a wholeness within his own separateness. He glimpsed the goal of creating within his consciousness, and then giving back to man the significant existence of the world.

Such a world would consist, then, of an accumulation of inter-related correspondences between outward objects and inner poetic realizations of them: objects which had become the highly personal symbols of his poetry.

The principle on which Rilke chose the fragments to fill up the gaps in himself was one of existence. He was looking for objects which exist, as his father and mother and perhaps he himself did not exist, and as, indeed, he trusted no one to exist. Works of art, jugs, towers, trees, unrequited lovers, heroes, Greek steles, these gradually won him over and healed him within their affirmations, and he gradually returned their beautiful gift by giving them new existence within his interior life. He made of them a world.

Rilke's world, though, has its own kind of unreality. He could not accept life as it is, or—should I say—as it is not. For in truth, consciousness is intermittent. Our selves are divided between mind and body, waking and sleep, dream and reality. We are parcelled out between conscious and unconscious, and torn apart by conflicting feelings. It is not even true to say that works of art in which master spirits have distilled the quintessence of thought or

3

mood really have a consistency which we lack. For they only find their existence within our existence, and as such are as subject to intermittency of consciousness as any other experience.

All the same, the idea of works of art and even of the way in which animals pursue their lives, not looking before and after, can console Rilke. Ultimately what he asks of life is that it should be merged into a single unity which we attribute to the dead. For when people are dead we think of them as symbols; the symbols of those qualities which we regard as the most essential in their lives. Rilke thought—he had to do so—life and death to be different sides of single existence, like the bright and dark sides of the moon. Death had to borrow from life its human love and wholeness, its presence among created things, while life had to borrow from death its symbolic truth. 'Only from the side of death,' (he wrote in 1920 to a young wife who had been forsaken: the letter is quoted in Appendix 2 of the Leishman-Spender translation), 'when death is not accepted as an extinction, but imagined as an altogether surpassing intensity, only from the side of death, I believe, is it possible to do justice to love.' And in a letter to his Polish translator (quoted in Leishman's notes to the same edition), he writes that 'Affirmation of life *and* affirmation of death reveal themselves as one. . . . The true form of life extends through BOTH regions, the blood of the mightiest circulation pulses through BOTH: THERE IS NEITHER A HERE NOR BEYOND BUT ONLY THE GREAT UNITY, in which the "Angels", those beings that surpass us, are at home.'

Rilke does not base these assertions on any authority but his own; and his own authority, as I have tried to demonstrate, rests on his psychological need . . . He tries to sever any connection between his ideas and the Christian myth, from which they originate, but to which they are in the relation of children who have renounced their parents.

> Transitoriness, he writes (again to his Polish translator) is everywhere plunged into a profound Being. And therefore all the forms of the here and now are not merely to be used in a time-limited way, but, so far as we can, instated within those superior significances in which we share. NOT, HOWEVER, IN THE CHRISTIAN SENSE (from which I more and more passionately

withdraw), but in a purely mundane, deeply mundane, blissfully mundane consciousness, to instate what is HERE seen and touched within the wider, within the widest orbit—that is what is required. Not within Beyond, whose shadow darkens the earth, but within a whole, within THE WHOLE.

It is necessary, I think, to question these ideas, not so much for the purpose of criticizing Rilke's poetry, but for that of understanding the development of modern literature today away from such highly individualistic envisionings. We can accept the fiction of the angels as an inspired symbol to express the functioning of art. We can accept the view that everything external has to be transformed into inner life: though with reservations, since it is arguable that such a process risks sacrificing one of the values of living, the sense of outsideness, otherness, that certain things should be impenetrable, unsymbolic of reference. It is necessary surely to insist that the whole universe should not be understood, be transformed into invisible inner world, and that a serious mistake of writers like Joyce, Proust, and Rilke has been to attempt too much transformation.

This, though, is a matter of critical disagreement. There is a more important objection where Rilke's poetic philosophy becomes quite unacceptable. This, surely, is in his version of death. He regards death as a sphere of existence into which he projects all his wishes for a continuity of being which he does not find in life. These thoughts, moreover, have very little to do with the reality of death. They are thoughts about the dead, which is another matter. Rilke reflects about heroes and unhappy lovers and saints—all of them dead—and thinks that he would like to fortify life with attributes that he bestows upon such purposive abstractions. He ties up attributes of heroes, lovers, and saints into a bundle, and calls it the unilluminated side of life which is death. This idea of death amounts either to a sense of purpose abstracted from the condition of living or simply to the subconscious. But neither of these, nor even the 'altogether surpassing intensity' with which the dead seem to persist in our thoughts, can truly create a reality of death which is outside the conditions of life.

One cannot accept his ideas about death, because death after all is real. The misuse of poetry which consists in transferring poetic ideas about the dead to death itself or the condition of being dead is a poeticization of reality—an offence he is often guilty of.

The angels, however, are a poetic invention which we can accept, because they clarify his attitude to reality without claiming that the poetic idea establishes the real. The angels are gigantic figures (borrowed perhaps from El Greco) in which outward reality fuses with inward significance. 'The angel', he wrote to his Polish translator, 'is the creature in whom the transformation of the visible into the invisible we are performing is already complete.' In another letter he recalls how when he was in Spain the landscape near Toledo developed to an extreme point in him his tendency to envisage objects demanding of him that he should make them part of himself, and transform them into his poetic world. 'Everywhere, appearance and vision came, as it were, together in the object, in every one of them a whole inner world was exhibited, as though an angel, in whom space was included, were blind and looking into himself.'

The angel, then, is a projection of the task which began originally with Rilke piecing his soul together out of experiences whose continuity he entered so passionately into. These experiences gradually demanded that he should bring to birth the invisibility of their existences within his own. The angel was the transformation of the task into a faith that there were forces in the world connecting the seen with the unseen, and making of the fusion language.

There is something terrifying about the concept of the isolated poet, acting as substitute-spiritual-institution, projecting into the world the idea of the angels, in whom the individual is made impersonal, isolated vision made objective. Rilke himself is terrified.

Yet the angels stand triumphantly at either end of the *Duino Elegies*, like the angels with flaming swords guarding the Garden of Eden. And the idea of their reality—the relating of everything else to their consistency—is what provides the inner form of the Elegies, which are a rather wild garden between these two gateways. For the inner form is really free association. Consistency of existence in the angels suggests the potential consistency of lovers and heroes. Such consistencies suggest their opposites, the inconsistency and fragmentariness of life. Life suggests dolls, and dolls works of art. Then there are certain subjects to be covered if this is to be a summation of a life-time's experiencing and thinking.

So at the opening of the First Elegy, there stands the great transforming machine of the angel, a figure of wonder and terror:

> Wer, wenn ich schriee, hörte mich denn aus der Engel
> Ordnungen? und gesetzt selbst, es nähme
> einer mich plötzlich ans Herz: ich verginge von seinem
> stärkeren Dasein. Denn das Schöne ist nichts
> als des Schreckichen Anfang, den wir noch grade ertragen,
> und wir bewundern es so, weil es gelassen verschmäht,
> uns zu zerstören. Ein jeder Engel ist schrecklich.

> Who, if I cried would hear me among the angelic
> order? And even if one of them suddenly
> pressed me against his heart, I should suddenly fade in the strength
>   of his
> stronger existence. For Beauty's nothing
> but beginning of Terror we're still just able to bear,
> and why we adore it so is because it serenely
> disdains to destroy us. Each single angel is terrible.

The angels are too terrible to apprehend, so the poet turns away from them and seeks human examples in which life has shown strength of existence. There are the lovers: the unrequited Gaspara Stampa who in Venice, in 1549, fell desperately in love with the young Collaltino, who deceived her. It is her unrequited passion which provides Rilke with the 'far intenser example of loving'. Requital, to him, is like the shattering of a pitcher. Then there are the heroes:

> denk: es erhält sich der Held, selbst der Untergang war ihm
> nur ein Vorwand, zu sein: seine letzte Geburt.

> Consider: the Hero continues, even his fall
> was a pretext for further existence, an ultimate birth.

There were saints who prayed

> dass sie der riesige Ruf
> aufhob vom Boden: sie aber Knieten
> Unmögliche, weiter und achtetens nicht

                        until the giant call
lifted them off the ground; yet they went impossibly
on with their kneeling, in undistracted attention.

Then he turns to legends and to works of art. To the origin of
song in the legend of Linos, to those Attic steles set over the graves
of the Grecian dead:

> war nicht Liebe und Abschied
> so leicht auf die Schultern gelegt, als wär es aus anderm
> Stoffe gemacht als bei uns.

> were not love and farewell
> so lightly laid upon shoulders, they seemed to be made
> of other stuff than with us.

Against these movements towards consistency, there is life
itself whose intermittency Rilke views with growing disgust.
There is the guilty river-god of the blood,

> O der dunkeler Wind seiner Brust aus gewundener Muschel

> Oh, the gloomy blast of his breast from the twisted shell!

Then there is the fact that we are never 'single-minded unper-
plexed', and that 'while we're intent on one thing, we feel the
cost and conquest of another'. Only in childhood, when alone,
we entertained ourselves with everlastingness.

One of the most persistent ideas in Rilke is that animals are
nearer the centre of existence than are we. Man sees only death,
while the animal moves into eternity. In front of us we always
have the world 'und niemals Nirgends ohne nicht' (and never
nowhere without no). The condition of our living is departure
from Here and Now. These considerations lead Rilke into those
areas where his subjectivity is perhaps most dangerous. For only
in the act of dying, or in the life within the womb, is man not
gazing at the centre of life from the outsideness of his own
consciousness. In the Eighth Elegy:

> Denn nah am Tod sieht man den Tod nicht mehr
> und starrt *hinaus*, vielleicht mit grossem Tierblick.

> Nearing death, one perceives death no longer,
> and stares ahead, perhaps with large brute gaze.

and then, at the opposite extreme of the womb, before birth:

> O seligkeit der kleinen Kreatur,
> die immer bleibt in Schoosse, der sie austrug.

> O bliss of tiny creatures that remain
> forever in the womb that brought them forth.

But the angel reconciles inner and outer worlds, while at the same time it objectivizes the subjective Rilkean task. It provides the gateways out of this world of the elegies where both I (ich) and thou (du) are always Rilke appealing to Rilke. Rilke could only escape from the subjectivity of an inner life of his own, into which he had taken all his experience and turned it into language of his own personal vision, by believing—with what faith—that this task of ingathering the world, naming it, and poetically creating it was an objective one. The triumph of his achievement was that at the end he should consider it was not just his. It was the world through him becoming world. It was performed by the angels.

Then he could cry in triumph that the earth was on his side: the transformation was complete:

> Erde, ist es nicht dies was du willst: unsichtbar
> in uns erstehn?—ist es dein Traum nicht,
> einmal unsichtbar zu sein?—Erde! unsichtbar!
> Was, wenn Verwandlung nicht, ist dein drängender Auftrag?

> Earth, isn't this what you want: an invisible
> re-arising in us? Is it not your dream
> to be one day invisible? Earth! invisible!
> What is your urgent command, if not transformation?

It is tempting to think that in the invention of the angels Rilke was returning to the catholicism of his childhood. His task was conceived of as a religious duty—the relating of the external world to spiritual life, and having undertaken it, he discovered that after all it was not just *his*: it belonged to the world. The concept of the angels even seems parallel to that of churches. Like church towers, these figures dominate the landscape, where they act as transforming machines mediating between the spiritual and the material. All the same, Rilke's repudiation of any such an interpretation of his symbol is explicit. And its force does not lie just in his pointing out that the angels are closer to Islamic than to Christian ones, but to the fact that—despite all that is mystical in him—they are projections of human values, and they are performing a human task. They are interpreting world and society to Man in a scheme where human existence is supposed to provide the wholeness.

★   ★   ★   ★

Nearly a quarter of a century after the publication of the *Duino Elegies* (which were begun in 1912, and completed ten years later) T. S. Eliot completed his *Four Quartets*. This poem has a relationship to its author's work and to his time which is parallel to the *Duino Elegies*. In *Four Quartets* Eliot, like Rilke, sets down his ideas about life and death, love and eternity. Like Rilke, too, he draws on a lifetime of experience, and the reader feels that *Four Quartets* is a testament in which all the poet has learned about life is concentrated and purified in order to express everything he has to say about it.

Having said that the two works have the same place in their authors' *œuvre*, it is necessary to say that in all other ways they seem as opposite as two works having similar aims could well be. To begin with, the worlds of the two poets are totally different. Rilke's world is inescapably the world of the 'I'. It is an enlarged 'I', a hollowed-out, capacious, three-dimensional 'I', transformed into a vessel which can hold the 'not-I'. But the experiences on which the work is constructed, the significance they have in the poetry, the idiom and the use of imagery are all Rilke's own, and have the unmistakable Rilkean attitudes which could only be his. When Rilke says 'you', he is appealing to his own experience and his own potentialities to experience still further. When he says 'we' in a sentence like 'Denn wir, wo wir fühlen, verflüchtigen' (For we, when we feel, evaporate) he is only forsaking the 'I' to the extent of appealing to the reader to enter into the Rilkean experience and accept its validity.

Of course, I do not mean that Rilke is an egotist, talking egotistically about himself. I mean that the principle he works on

is that only by absorbing all experience into himself can he transform it into what is beyond himself. The world is given back to
the world only after he has suffered it within the process of his
imagination. The task of the self can, indeed, finally be transferred
to the angels. All the same, the angels are not, as I have pointed
out, orthodox. They are projections of an individualizing process
into the idea of a task beyond individuality.

Eliot most decidedly renounces the method of Rilke. There are
passages of *Four Quartets* which seem even an answer to him. The
key passage in which he rejects the personalist approach and points
to his own is:

> You are not here to verify
> Instruct yourself or inform curiosity
> Or carry report. You are here to kneel
> Where prayer has been valid.

Rilke's whole position rests on the witnessing power of experience. He pieces together his soul out of fragments of outside
reality deeply experienced (the torso of the Archaic Apollo, for
example), and finally he discovers a means to get beyond himself
by, as it were, experiencing his own idea of the experience of
lovers, heroes, saints, etc. But Eliot writes—in one of his more
sententious passages:

> There is, it seems to us,
> At best, only a limited value
> In the knowledge derived from experience.
> The knowledge imposes a pattern, and falsifies,
> For the pattern is new in every moment
> And every moment is a new and shocking
> Valuation of all we have been.

The Rilkean idea is to fulfil the interior pattern of the individual, which achieves its fruition in a personal, separate death, a
death unlike that of anyone else. For Eliot, on the contrary, the
task of life, and of his poetry, is to enter into and conform with
an already existing pattern which has nothing to do with self.
You have to go by the way of dispossession (which means, above
all, dispossession of the self) in order to arrive at the place where
you started, that is to say, at the point in the pattern which existed
before you were born.

The difference is, then, that Eliot believes in a pre-established outside pattern, which is the true significance of both past and future and of the lives of the living and the dead, to which it is the duty of those living in the present to make the future conform. An ideal condition would be one in which there was neither past nor future, but a continuous present where men were absorbed in living the pattern imposed by the past and which—if they lived in this way—would admit of no heterodox future.

Eliot does not, however, think of the pattern as static. In fact, he strains his imagination in the endeavour to make us enter into the idea of a non-fixed pattern where past and future co-exist in a continual present:

> At the still—point of the turning world, Neither flesh nor fleshness ;
> Neither from nor towards; at the still point, there the dance is,
> But neither arrest nor movement. And do not call it fixity.
> Where past and future are gathered. Neither movement from nor
>   towards,
> Neither ascent nor decline. Except for the point, the still point,
> There would be no dance, and there is only the dance.
> I can only say, *there* we have been: but I cannot say where.
> And I cannot say, how long, for that is to place it in time.

and :
>   History may be servitude,
> History may be freedom. See, now they vanish,
> The faces and places, with the self which, as it could, loved them,
> To become renewed, transfigured, in another pattern.

In Eliot's view, then, an outside pattern, which is also outside time, impinges on present existence, and it is the duty of those living in the present to participate in the dance of the pattern. At the same time, reservations are made to distinguish such a view from those Eastern philosophies which commit the devout to a condition of complete unliving within life :

> Yet the enchainment of past and future
> Woven in the weakness of the changing body,
> Protects mankind from heaven and damnation
> Which flesh cannot endure.

Unlike Eastern mystics, then, we accept 'the protection' of our living bodies against exposure to the intolerable reality of either

heaven or hell, which would absorb us completely into themselves.
Eliot is equally careful to distinguish his idea of the pattern from
the reactionary view of life:

> We cannot revive old factions
> We cannot restore old policies
> Or follow an antique drum.

One of the achievements of *Four Quartets*, indeed, is to express
in poetry not only a vision of orthodoxy (it is more this than an
orthodox vision, because in some ways Eliot's religion is surely a
very peculiar mixture of Christianity and Buddhism), but also
the responsible scruples of his extremely conscientious mind. He
is a more scrupulous thinker in his poetry even than in his
prose. Without misinterpreting it, there is nothing in *Four
Quartets*, for example, which could give comfort to political
totalitarians.

But even if we make allowance for a few concessions to the
values of being alive and of human love, there is little in *Four
Quartets* which suggests that Eliot's vision of orthodoxy could be
interpreted into terms of the present direction of civilization. By
this, I don't just mean that if we were to live lives devoted to fulfilling a pre-established pattern of being which is outside time, we
would have to scrap most of our machinery (because machinery
above all produces the illusion of progress, and gives us the vivid
impression that the present day has outdistanced past history). I
mean something different: that if there is any hope for our civilization it lies in extending and developing the concept of human
love. The love which is outside time, and which is the radiance of
the dance in *Four Quartets*, will not persuade us to use modern
techniques to help men who are starving. It is not inconsistent
with doing so, but the interpretation of Eliot's ideas into action
taking place within history seems impossibly difficult. I know
this objection will seem naïve, but it may none the less be
serious. There is a paradox at the centre of Eliot's system. It is
anti-individualistic, and yet surely it tends to cultivate individuals, even if these are individuals who devote their lives to
shedding their individuality in order to enter into the pattern
of the dance. Moreover, I doubt whether any philosophy which

denigrates the simple and sensuous values of being alive will ever lead men to do much for the living.

*   *   *   *

The *Duino Elegies* are one of the outlying points of the excesses of the individual vision. And like so many other modern works, Rilke seems to have gone in a direction where only he could go, and beyond which no poet coming after him can go further. The idea of the angels, for example, is ultimate. The angels symbolize the concept of the individual poet's task of transforming the outer world into his own inner invisibility at a point where it has become scarcely tolerable, for *him*: so he has to throw it out, projected as the idea of an objective task, dominating the modern human landscape. All the same, Rilke is preoccupied with life. Compared with *Four Quartets*, the *Duino Elegies* is an area densely populated with humanity: lovers, heroes, acrobats, and all the inhabitants of the fair in the Tenth Elegy. Love, happiness, and suffering are surprisingly real in Rilke's consciousness. And the idea that a world has to be transformed is immensely present, even if the reader may feel that the angels are machines of individualist vision doomed rapidly to become extinct. It still remains to be seen whether orthodoxy can do as much for the sad condition of modern humanity.

The completed *Four Quartets* was published in 1944. The shift of emphasis from the *Duino Elegies* to *Four Quartets* is surely significant of a change in the spirit of humanity during the past quarter-century. The *Duino Elegies* were the last great outpouring of a supremely individualist era. The poet looked on the external world as a system of symbolic experiences whose significance could be created within the subjective experience of his poetry. He thought that the Christian orthodoxies could no longer perform the task of turning the visible phenomena of industrialized society into the invisible spirit.

This was a phase in which the poet became a kind hero to many: Rilke was the last of such heroes. And the *Duino Elegies* was perhaps the last major achievement of a movement that has already passed into history.

IV

PERSONAL RELATIONS AND
PUBLIC POWERS

E. M. FORSTER would repudiate the suggestion that he is
a visionary. He has a vision—perhaps more than one—but
lacks the absoluteness of writers like Rimbaud, Rilke, or D. H.
Lawrence. He lacks the sense that if the world cannot be transformed into terms of his vision, then all may be lost. He hedges
his beliefs round with many qualifications, and sometimes gives
the impression that any cause that is worthwhile must inevitably
be an almost-lost one. Nor does he care for causes anyway. He is
conscious of two kinds of truth. One is Truth with a big T which
men sometimes think they glimpse, and the other is the truth
about the Truth. The truth about it being that it can only be
glimpsed.

His vision has centre, but he doubts its power to affect the circumference. Indeed he is sceptical of every claim that the centre
can change the world, and he reverts often to the idea that it should
have no pretensions to do so. He admits to belief in love, but not
in the Republic of Love ('Democracy is not a Beloved Republic
really, and never will be'), and the belief he outlines in his essay
What I Believe is so much a criticism of belief in general that
it is easy to see it as just this, and ignore what he believes in
particular:

> I do not believe in Christianity because I think that Christians
> deceive people when they pretend that the world can be governed
> by Christian principles. What I really believe in is the moral and
> aesthetic and humane sensibility of a few enlightened people who
> are to be found scattered about in all nations and classes. However,
> I only mention in a whisper that I believe this, because to say it

out loud would be encouraging you to think that such people may perhaps influence the development of history, and I do not believe they can.

He believes, though, in the whisper; and he is opposed to 'saying it out loud' not just because people may be disappointed when they discover that the 'chosen few' are ineffective, but because the whisper loses its own kind of truth and force by being said aloud. He is unwilling to hear the advice of the world, and left cold by those who think they are going to influence it. His still centre is not the turning point of the world, but just a still centre. One can believe in it—or should I say in *them* who are *there*?—just the same.

In *The Longest Journey* Ansell, who has betrayed nothing, exclaims furiously to Rickie, who has betrayed much, when Rickie is trying to justify himself by appealing to the situation of the great world:

> 'Where is the great world? There is no great world at all, only a little earth, for ever isolated from the rest of the little solar system. The little earth is full of tiny societies, and Cambridge is one of them. All the societies are narrow, but some are good and some are bad—just as one house is beautiful inside and another ugly. . . . The good societies say, "I tell you to do this because I am Cambridge." The bad ones say, "I tell you to do that because I am the great world"—not because I am "Peckham", or "Billingsgate", or "Park Lane", but "because I am the great world". They lie.'

And in the essay *What I Believe* from which I have already quoted, he tells us that he believes only in faith with a little f. Sometimes he may seem discouraging by reminding us of our weakness, until we recollect that he is also warning us against worse weakness: that of false optimism. More, he is pointing us to where, within the general weakness, we may assert the particular strength. He conducts a guerilla warfare on three fronts. He resists—with a deceptive air of ineffectiveness—the crudely powerful methods of business and politics; he rejects the simplifications of spiritual salvationism, whether in religion or in art; and he reinforces human relations and solitude.

He insists, too, on the double aspect of things: that Faith with a big F may fail if it deceives the faithful into thinking that they can govern the world by Christian principles; but that with a little f it may enable one to stick to one's friends and to enjoy the better rather than the worse life. He says that he hopes that if he were called on to choose between his country and his friend he would choose his friend; and he invokes Dante placing Brutus and Cassius in the lowest circle of hell because they had chosen to betray their friend Julius Caesar rather than their country Rome, as justification for the preference. If Forster could contemplate martyrdom, it would be for the particular rather than for some general principle.

Forster is criticized by social revolutionaries for being wishy-washy and, of course, by the orthodox for his lack of a fixed and stated metaphysical belief. It is important, therefore, to emphasize that he is uncompromising about personal and aesthetic values. He habitually characterizes democracy, revolution, social justice, history, and religion as a 'mess'. But at the centre of the mess he sees everywhere, there are one or two things which are hard and irreducible.

Personal relations are the centre of his vision. But they are not without implications which produce in his novels the concentric circles of a human comedy including hell, purgatory, and paradise. Within the little world, within the particular relationship, within solitude even, there are the infernal fires, as well as Purgatory and Paradise. Henry Wilcox, when the mask has been torn away and he is revealed as faithless to his wife in spirit and body—and to all she loved, which is worse—wins his way back into the circle of human relations and into the heart of Margaret Schlegel. Hell is the 'panic and emptiness' under the surface crust of a life based on power, social position, and things. Paradise is perhaps the mysterious beauty which Mrs. Wilcox discovers in her house Howards End, and perhaps it is also the understanding between Dr. Aziz and Mrs. Moore when they meet for the first time in the Moslem mosque, although this lasts only a moment.

The Comedy of Forster's world is not the *Divine Comedy*, and still less Balzac's Human one. Forster would recall that the *Divine Comedy* itself, after all, is a metaphor, and his own—which might be called the Human-and-Divine one—is a metaphor of a metaphor, where it owes something to Dante. All the same, to remember that Forster admires Dante, and Beethoven, and even has praise for Wagner, is to remind ourselves that his confined world of tiny societies is formidable.

His characters who seem touched with sublimity are alone, and their relationship with others is of understanding them rather than communing with them. Mrs. Wilcox leaves Howards End to Helen Schlegel, but she does so without there being an explicit relationship between the two women. Mrs. Moore likes Dr. Aziz, but she withdraws into a mystery of solitude at the time when he is wrongly accused of assaulting Miss Quested, her prospective daughter-in-law, in the Marabar caves—this although she knows him to be innocent, and might have said so. And Dr. Aziz, aware that Mrs. Moore might have helped him, and did not, still thinks meeting her in the temple the most beautiful event of his life, but it has become part of his solitude and ceased to be a relationship.

Awareness of a final mystery in which not the religions but the religious meet is perhaps the ultimate and most lonely of the little centres. But even an experience of Truth with a big T is subject to the truth about the Truth. God evades us even if we cannot avoid Him. In the mosque:

> Mrs. Moore felt that she had made a mistake in mentioning God, but she found him increasingly difficult to avoid as she grew older, and he had been constantly in her thoughts since she entered India, though oddly enough he satisfied her less. She must needs pronounce his name frequently, as the greatest she knew, yet she had never found it less efficacious. Outside the arch there seemed always an arch, beyond the remotest echo silence.

There is not always even silence, sometimes there is mockery. In the Marabar caves there is a mysterious echo—which has the effect of making every statement, however significant, return to the listener as—Boum! This echo, which Mrs. Moore as well as Miss Quested heard during their visit to the caves, has the effect of ridiculing and dwarfing the vastness of Mrs. Moore's vision of the universe which had opened up so wonderfully on her arrival in India.

> Visions are supposed to entail profundity, but—wait till you get one, dear reader! The abyss also may be petty, the serpent of

eternity made of maggots; her constant thought was: 'Less attention should be paid to my daughter-in-law in future and more to
me, there is no sorrow like my sorrow.' But pettiness here has its
usefulness. . . .

Because in the cave she had perceived 'something snub-nosed,
incapable of generosity—the undying worm itself—'

the echo which made Mrs. Moore mean and jealous also made her
conclude that the question of whether or not her future daughter-
in-law, Adela, had been sexually assaulted was of less importance
than the British thought, when rigging the trial of Aziz in the name
of morals. 'All this fuss over a frightened girl!' Nothing had happened, 'and if it had', she found herself thinking with the cynicism
of a withered priestess, 'if it had, there are worse evils than love'.
The unspeakable attempt presented itself to her as love: in a cave,
in a church—Boum, it amounts to the same.

Or sometimes there is a question, with a vague indication of a
smile as answer. In the Hindu ceremony at the court of the Rajah,
described so elaborately towards the end of *A Passage to India*, the
poets of the State had composed inscriptions for the occasion.
These were

hung where they could not be read, or had twitched their drawing
pins out of the stucco, and one of them (composed in English to
indicate his universality) consisted, by an unfortunate slip of the
draughtsman, of the words, 'God si Love'.

'God si Love. Is this the first message of India?' And returning to
the theme, in a later passage, he reflects:

'God si Love!' There is fun in heaven. God can play practical
jokes upon Himself, draw chairs away from beneath His own
posteriors, set His own turbans on fire, and steal His own petti-
coats when he bathes. By sacrificing good taste, this worship
achieves what Christianity shirked: the inclusion of merriment.
All spirit as well as all matter must participate in salvation, and if
practical jokes are banned, the circle is incomplete.

Perhaps Forster also thinks that the circle and its centre can
never be drawn or placed, or that if, for a moment, they are defined, they shift away the next moment somewhere else. One of

his most famous scenes is the opening of *The Longest Journey*, when Rickie Elliott and his friend Ansell discuss philosophy in Rickie's Cambridge rooms. Ansell takes up a pencil and draws a square, and within the square a circle, 'and within the circle a square, and inside that another circle, and inside that another circle, and inside that another square'. 'Why will you do that?' Rickie asks. No answer. 'Are they real?' 'The inside one is—the one in the middle of everything that there's never room enough to draw.'

The focusing point of the vision of life in these novels is the innermost centre of an innermost square which cannot be drawn. This is neither so discouraging nor so whimsical as it sounds. There is a relationship between squares and circles: perhaps a shifting one, but it can, as it were, be caught on the wing and defined for the moment when it is valid. Forster also prefers small circles—the ones nearest the innermost—to large ones. He believes too that relations can be established between states that are defined. You can connect.

That he sees mystery at the centre of things does not make him a mystic. Nor, certainly, is he a dogmatist who believes that relations are either fixed or refer back to a fixed rule which men should obey. Nor does he take pleasure in authoritarian irrationality like Kafka, who sees a kind of purposive purposelessness everywhere, an authority which gives the wrong orders and is yet infinitely to be respected. The centre of Forster's vision is, really, love, but it is love which only attains definition within a relationship. Since everything depends on the right relationship, then what may be love in one situation may not be in another. The nature of these relations is essentially moral. There are moral situations, not fixed rules. On the whole Forster appears to think that people who go about the business of life following fixed rules destroy the capacity for love in themselves, and may even end (like Mr. Wilcox) by behaving in ways which are demonstrably immoral. But even this is not a rule, because there are no certain rules, but only imagination, perception, courage, and feeling. In Forster's world there are not fixed morals, but there are virtues, perhaps because virtues tend to set you in the right direction.

Forster's novels are comedies of moral inconsistency. Within the inconsistency, nevertheless, it is possible, in given situations, to judge certain acts. When the Herritons, in *Where Angels Fear to Tread*, go out to Italy to extract the child of their English relation from the Italian, Gino Carella, who has behaved so badly to his wife that she has died, they are fortified by feelings about the moral rightness of their cause. What proves them wrong is not the superior moral character of Gino, who though warm and attractive is in most ways an unscrupulous rascal, but the little scene where Gino is looking at the baby, which is seated on his knee. At that moment Gino is at the centre of the circle. His feeling for the child proves the Herritons wrong. And after this, when they steal the child, not only does the baby die in the accident which follows on the theft, but also Philip Herriton is later to discover that his own happiness has been ruined.

So if there aren't rules, nevertheless there are perhaps directions, tendencies, which indicate, rather than describe, the moral quality of conduct. He has been criticized for dividing his characters too much into the sheep and the goats—the good Schlegels, the bad Wilcoxes, the good Mrs. Moore and Aziz, the bad Anglo-Indian officials. And it is true that the action of his comedies is based on the idea of a game between teams: the Schlegels versus the Wilcoxes, with Leonard Bast in between as football, if you like. Certain of his characters seem endowed with the quality of 'grace' (Stephen Wonham may strike one as unduly so favoured by his inventor). Mrs. Wilcox is the kind of character to whom the reader grants an unchallenged overdraft of moral credit. At a certain point he might feel inclined to look closely at Mrs. Moore's securities.

Then there are those who, without grace, are felt to be genuinely well-meaning, and possessed of enough intelligence not to be paving hell with their good intentions: Philip Herriton, Margaret Schlegel, and Cyril Fielding. But there are also those who waver: Helen Schlegel, Adela Quested, and Gino Carella.

It would be a fault in Forster to divide his characters into teams if in doing so he permitted his moral feelings to prejudice his observation of life. Balzac and Dickens, for instance, are sometimes criticized for making their 'good' characters so good that they become flat figures simply illustrating a moral thesis (though I

doubt whether this criticism illustrates more than a curious prejudice of our psychoanalytical time that there can be no simple
and good people because everyone must have 'repressions' and
'complexes'). But with Forster the distribution of qualities among
his characters is evidently influenced by what he thinks not about
morals but about people. He believes in an aristocracy of those
who understand; and in the baseness of those who are defective in
imagination and feeling—those who have what Lionel Trilling
has so excellently analysed as 'uneducated hearts'.

In Forster's world, people have the tendency to move in a good
or a bad, an upward or a downward direction. But the characteristic moral situation is not right people against wrong people, but
the moment of revelation. Such moments are just as likely to
occur to the characters who are goats as to those who are sheep.
Adela Quested has a tremendous one in the trial of Aziz when,
suddenly gifted with perfectly clear memory of the excursion to
the caves, she answers 'I am not quite sure', to the question
whether anyone followed her into the particular cave where, until
now, she has imagined herself to have been assaulted. Rickie
Elliott has one when he chances on Gerald Dawes and Agnes
Pembroke clasped in one another's arms in the clearing in the
wood. Then after Gerald dies in the football match Rickie, in a
moment of power, forces Agnes to the centre of the circle of her
grief: 'It's the worst thing that can ever happen to you in all your
life, and you've got to mind it—you've got to mind it. They'll
come saying, "Bear up—trust to time." No, no; they're wrong.
Mind it.'

A moral action in these novels is a kind of explosion, a setting
off of accumulated forces by a test. The orthodox, of course, will
—and do—protest that the judgement which occurs in the explosion is arbitrary, or sentimental, depending on a vague mysticism
about 'life'. This is not the case. For someone, in a moment of
crisis, to act in the right way or to feel the right thing in a Forster
novel, means the triumph of values which are realized in the
action. Affection, truth (with a small t); respect for passion (in
the physical as well as the spiritual sense); love of aesthetic beauty;
reverence for the past; freedom: these are a few of the qualities,
like rays, that do converge to a bursting centre when, for example,

Miss Quested speaks up and tells the truth, or Miss Bartlett turns out to be the ally of Lucy Honeychurch and George Emerson, or Miss Avery comes out of the garden with the sword.

Henry Wilcox's last failure is in his dealings with Helen Schlegel, his sister-in-law (for he is now married to Margaret), towards the end of *Howards End*. Assuming that because she has been rather inexplicably in Munich for eight months, she must be physically—and perhaps mentally—ill, he arranges with Maragret to trap her at Howards End. This scheme does not succeed, because Margaret, seeing her sister at the deserted house, has a moment of revulsion against her husband's tactics, and sends him away, together with the doctor they have brought with them. She justifies her action to her husband:

> 'It all turns on affection now,' said Margaret. 'Affection. Don't you see?' Resuming her usual methods, she wrote the word on the house with her finger. 'Surely you see. I like Helen very much, you not so much. Mr. Mansbridge doesn't know her. That's all. And affection, when reciprocated, gives rights. Put that down in your note-book, Mr. Mansbridge. It's a useful formula.'

The doctor, who has seen Helen for a moment, informs Henry Wilcox that she is pregnant. A few inquiries from Margaret reveal that her sister is not married. Later, Margaret requests from her husband that she and her sister be allowed to spend one night together at the deserted house of Howards End, before Helen returns to the Continent. Henry refuses. This stupidity causes Margaret to heap on him the account of all his actions :

> 'You shall see the connection if it kills you, Henry! You have had a mistress—I forgave you. My sister has a lover—you drive her from the house. Do you see the connection? Stupid, hypocritical, cruel—oh, contemptible!—a man who insults his wife when she's alive and cants with her memory when she's dead. A man who ruins a woman for his pleasure, and casts her off to ruin other men. And gives bad financial advice, and then says he is not responsible. These, man, are you. You can't recognize them, because you cannot connect. . . .'

Shortly before giving this account of Henry's misdemeanours, she has appealed to him to forgive her sister: 'Will you forgive her—as you hope to be forgiven, and as you have actually been forgiven? Forgive her for one night only. That will be enough.'

It may be argued that a tremendous weight is here being put on personal relations. It is indeed the weight of the Christian ethic, with the forgiveness of the Lord's Prayer and the teaching of Divine Love, which connects. Forster has detached the Christian teaching from the circumference of the churches and concentrated it into the nucleus of the personal relationship.

He does not, however, like D. H. Lawrence, make a doctrine of relations between individuals. The whisper is tremendous, but it does not rise to a shout, and the element of salvationism which it certainly contains is restrained by a stoic awareness that one cannot expect too much of the truth. Personal relations are above all an act of recognition between those who form a kind of secret human aristocracy:

> the aristocracy of the sensitive, the considerate, the plucky. Its members are to be found in all nations and classes, and all through the ages, and there is a secret understanding between them when they meet. They represent the true human tradition, the one permanent victory of our queer race over cruelty and chaos. Thousands of them perish in obscurity, a few are great names. They are sensitive for others as well as themselves, they are considerate without being fussy, their pluck is not swankiness but the power to endure; and they can take a joke.

They (personal relations) imply affection, loyalty, and sometimes a sharing of values which amounts to shared vision, or—as the Schlegels would put it—'speaking the same language'. However, individuals can respect different values in one another. Tastes that on the surface seem different may, when they are melted in the warmth of the personal, be identical. Thus Ansell recognizes qualities which make him love the Greek classics in Stephen Wonham, to whom a book is only bound-up sheets of paper between covers having certain measurements. In fact, Stephen Wonham, like the small boy in *The Celestial Omnibus*, is the embodiment of some aspect of Greece—and some scholars are the last to recognize this. . . . So personal relations are the basis for reconciliation between attitudes which—when stated in terms of doctrine—seem irreconcilable. Moslem and Christian are one when Mrs. Moore and Aziz meet in the mosque, and agnostic Hindu and Moslem, when Fielding and Aziz join in the celebrations at the court of the maharajah. This is where Forster's whisper might usefully be heeded by statesmen and churchmen.

Personal relations, however, run into the tragic (where Forster is reluctant to follow them) when social forms and edicts interfere. And Forster, who may be said to have traced the hidden path of a way of life in our society, for a quarter of a century, abandons the trail in 1924, with the last page of *A Passage to India*, where Aziz and Fielding reluctantly agree (but not without a kind of fierce joy on the part of Aziz, and of the Indian landscape) that the British Raj is a barrier preventing their friendship:

> 'India a nation! What an apotheosis! Last comer to the drab nineteenth-century sisterhood! Waddling in at this hour of the world to take her seat! She, whose only peer was the Holy Roman Empire, she shall rank with Guatemala and Belgium perhaps!' Fielding mocked again. And Aziz in an awful rage danced this way and that, not knowing what to do, and cried: 'Down with the English anyhow. That's certain. Clear out, you fellows, double quick, I say. We may hate one another, but we hate you most. If I don't make you go, Ahmed will, Karem will, if it's fifty-five hundred years we shall get rid of you, yes, we shall drive every blasted Englishman into the sea, and then'—he rode against him furiously—'and then,' he concluded, half kissing him, 'you and I shall be friends.'
>
> 'Why can't we be friends now?' said the other, holding him affectionately. 'It's what I want. It's what you want.'
>
> But the horses didn't want it—they swerved apart; the earth didn't want it, sending up rocks through which riders must pass single file; the temples, the tank, the jail, the palace, the birds, the carrion, the Guest House, that came into view as they issued from the gap and saw Mau beneath: they didn't want it, they said in their hundred voices, 'No, not yet,' and the sky said, 'No, not there.'

The forces that hinder proved to be stronger and vaster than India or the British Raj, and destruction of personal values has

increased rather than lessened with the decline of the British
Empire. Visiting India again, in 1946, Forster records :

> The big change I noticed was interest in politics. You cannot
> understand the modern Indians unless you realize that, politics
> occupy them passionately and constantly, that artistic problems,
> and even social problems—yes, even economic problems—are
> subsidiary. Their attitude is 'first we must find the correct political
> solution, and then we can deal with other matters.' I think the
> attitude is unsound, and used to say so; still, there it is, and they
> hold it much more vehemently than they did a quarter-century
> ago. When I spoke about the necessity of form in literature and
> the importance of the individual vision, their attention wandered,
> although they listened politely. Literature, in their view, should
> expound or inspire a political creed.

What Forster noticed about Indians is an attitude that today
affects the whole world, the West as well as the East. It is this
development of the world towards total politics which might
have turned another writer with his point of view into a tragedian,
if not into a total pessimist of anti-Vision, like George Orwell,
whose despairing novel *1984* appears to express very much
Forster's own view of the world today. Forster, however, has
declined to depress us by painting pictures of humanity in which
his central values can only be destroyed or become tragic. Instead,
since 1924, he has confined himself to making observations and
protests, and fighting for the better against the worse. He has
refused the role of apocalyptic prophet.

His silence is, perhaps, eloquent. For personal relations, unlike
less human values, are not realised by discouragement and
defeat. One who cares more for his friends than any cause or aim
would hesitate to write a book like Orwell's. And the tragic view
of life is the view that idea, ideals, or abstract form can emerge
from a human situation and become more real than those who
participate in it.

This is the view of Yeats when he writes: 'A moonlit or a starlit
dome disdains / All that man is, / All mere complexities / The
fury and the mire of human veins.' It is not a view which would
have much appeal to Forster, though he might admire it in Yeats.
He would prefer the simply stated admission between Aziz and

Fielding that their friendship cannot survive until . . . He sums up the attitude in *What I Believe*, from which I have already quoted:

> I am out of sympathy with the historic forces of my epoch, whether these are the power of the rulers or the revolt of the oppressed. I realize that this means I have cut myself off from the most powerful-seeming life and faith of my time. But I believe there is value in being truthful, in defining one's little sphere of interest and trying to relate it to the larger things.

'The little sphere', the centre, the circle within the square are metaphors he constantly comes back to. He has created a fictitious world where the forces of power—the Wilcoxes and the Anglo-Indians—are wonderfully balanced against the forces representing personal values—the Schlegels and Fielding with Aziz. The Wilcoxes and the Anglo-Indians are criticized for their failure to connect their business and politics with its effect in terms of lives which they control. This criticism is largely just, yet one may feel that there is another connection which Forster himself does not make explicit, though he is certainly aware of it. This is the connection between the freedom of action of the Schlegels—and even of Fielding—and the activities of Wilcoxes and Anglo-Indians. For ultimately the Schlegels can go on as they do, because they are living on unearned incomes obtained for them by the Wilcoxes. And Fielding was in India thanks to the British army.

This criticism does not invalidate the attacks made on business men and imperialists by the free agents whom their wealth and power has produced. It complicates the situation, however, by suggesting that Wilcoxes deserve a certain amount of credit for producing Schlegels, and that Forster's extremely penetrating picture of India in the 1920's would have had still more worth if he had indicated that the relationship between Fielding and Aziz, although frustrated by, was also the result of British power.

Within its limits, Forster's world seems to me almost complete. But it is limited, and perhaps the limitation is his failure to establish a missing link between the good results of wealth and power and the bad means used to obtain it. His good characters either do no work and live on unearned incomes, or the work they do is of some professional kind, like schoolmastering or scholarship, which, being much the same within all social systems, is untainted by power and economics. Perhaps the most devastating remark Margaret Schlegel makes to Henry, when she has become Mrs. Wilcox, is to taint him with not having been a soldier. It may occur to the reader that this remark strikes oddly in *Howards End*, because it is outside the context of Forster's world, where soldiers are all Blimps, very faintly coated with a thin sugar of good intentions. There is no study in all his characters of an administrator seriously divided between public and private conscience. The Anglo-Indian types, like the Wilcoxes, are certainly convincing, yet it is a defect that Forster has never invented a character in which his two worlds, the public and private, connect and meet on a high level of explicitness and conscience. Perhaps Ronnie in *Howards End* is an attempt to portray such a character, but Ronnie is too weak-kneed for the conflict in his nature between private and public loyalties to be illuminating. Yet administrators who love the arts and are aware of the importance of personal relations do exist, and for a true portrayal of middle-class life it is necessary to describe them.

The result of this limiting of what is really a wider problem to a personal sphere, more or less completely cut off from its basis of power, is the curious unreality of the last scene in *Howards End*. The redemption—within the sphere of personal relations—of Henry Wilcox is achieved, it will be remembered, in the scene where Henry, Margaret, Helen, and Helen's illegitimate baby by Leonard Bast (whom Charles Wilcox has accidentally killed in the course of punishing him for his 'seduction' of Helen) are all together in a hayfield. On the personal level this is credible. But so many social skeletons rattle in the cupboards of *Howards End* that the reader, surely, finds this conclusion almost irrelevant. Far better is the admitted defeat of Aziz and Fielding at the end of *A Passage to India*, though even this appears to me to be on a different plane of reality from the rest of the novel. One accepts nine-tenths of the argument: but there remains a protest in the reader's mind that Aziz and Fielding need not admit to such a defeat.

Forster has, though, stated very clearly certain values of the inner life. He leaves his readers with the impression that personal values cannot solve the problems of society, and society cannot tolerate personal values. Yet perhaps the very negativeness of this conclusion suggests its opposite: that they can, and must. And just as personal values can only be stated in a whisper, so perhaps the suggestion is the more valuable because it jumps out of his work, without his having made it. Irony, as several critics have pointed out, is an almost inevitable result of the situation of modern literature—and perhaps irony may sometimes even be unconscious. So that when Forster tells us of his discouragement in the face of the powerful-seeming forces and faiths of the present day, we may take leave to be encouraged, without quite knowing whether the irony is his, our own, or even implicit in the situations he describes.

He has held up to his time a mirror which reflects in his art a picture of civilized values achieved within small societies—Cambridge, the Schlegels, Fielding and Aziz. The values which these characters share owe something to the antiquity whose myths haunt most of his short stories, a good deal to the Keats of *The Ode on a Grecian Urn* and the sonnet on Homer. Most of all, though, Forster's characters are civilized by knowing, tolerating, enjoying, and disciplining their own natures. He has presented values of human personality in their weakness as well as their strength, and he has refused to compromise them with methods of power politics. In the long run perhaps he clarifies and strengthens immensely our conception of human individuals by showing that they are weak in relation to public power. They are weak—we see—because they would weaken their own humanity by accepting the terms on which it is possible to be strong.

Unless we are moving towards the completely inhuman existence of a world totally conditioned by power politics, then the almost ideal vision of human individuals, and relations between them, which burns through Forster's novels, is one which people may turn to the more passionately just because it is uncontaminated.

V

PIONEERING THE INSTINCTIVE LIFE

We, dear reader, you and I, we were born corpses and we are corpses. I doubt if there is even one of us who has ever known so much as an apple, a whole apple. All we know is shadows, even of apples. Shadows of everything, of the whole world, shadows even of ourselves. We are inside the tomb, and the tomb is wide and shadowy like hell, even if sky-blue by optimistic paint, so we think it is all the world. But our tomb is a wide tomb, full of ghosts, replicas. We are all spectres, we have not been able to touch even so much as an apple. Spectres we are to one another. Spectre you are to me, spectre I am to you. Shadow you are even to yourself. And by shadow I mean idea, concept, the abstracted reality, the ego. We are not solid, we don't live in the flesh. Our instincts and intuitions are dead, we live wound round with the winding sheet of abstraction. And the touch of anything solid hurts us. For our instincts and intuitions, which are our feelers of touch and knowing through touch, they are dead, amputated. We walk and talk and eat and copulate and laugh and evacuate wrapped in our winding-sheets, all the time wrapped in our winding-sheets.

THIS, from the *Introduction* to his paintings, puts the situation of human consciousness in our time, as Lawrence saw it. It is the situation in which all experience becomes an abstraction within the greater abstraction that is our idea of the state of the civilization in which we live. The tendency of modern literature has been for writers to relate particular spheres of individual vision to this larger condition, the small shadow to the larger shadow. Within the shadow-kingdom of the historically-doomed civilization, they have tried to set memories in order—Proust's recovery of time past, Eliot's arranging the fragments of his ruins.

Lawrence's work is above all a revolt against the idea that the consciousness of civilized men is an *object* of the civilization in which they live, which, in turn, is an object of the present phase of history. He is forever proclaiming that before all else he is a man, with a physical body and an instinctive life, and that although his body and instincts exist *within* civilization they are not the products *of* its condition at our particular moment of history. His work is a grand refusal of an intellectual attitude which has become so universal that to reject it may appear to be a rejection of the intellect itself. What Lawrence protested against was not intellect but the kind of intellectualization whereby men create a shadow-world for themselves. Men develop, for example, a theory about the state of civilization, and then regard the flesh and blood, natural scenery, and stone buildings around them as ideas or symbols illustrating the conclusion they have come to. Long before cities are ruined, we have made metal ruins of them, and ghosts of ourselves.

Lawrence was essentially a dialectician, a preacher rather than a prophet, fighting his time with methods and arguments chosen to surprise and take his enemy (everyone!) off guard. Like all preachers he defended a position which was reasonable by appealing not to reason but to realities which most of the reasonable of his time chose to ignore. The religious preacher is concerned primarily with proving to his audience out of their own experience that they have souls which know God. Reasoning comes after he has widened the field of discussion to areas which the irreligious refuse to accept, and then it takes place on ground whose existence they have denied. Lawrence was also concerned with widening the field of discussion by appealing to our experience, in order to demonstrate that civilization is not just our idea of the contemporary condition of the West. It is also our lives, and our lives are not simply intellectual; still less are they mental concepts about ourselves. Our lives, besides being 'The West in the twentieth century', are our physical bodies, the instinctual forces in us, and our relations with one another. If this could be proved by appealing to experience, then he could go on to say that there is a real outsideness of the world around us and not just the mental condition of our history.

In terms of our culture and civilization Lawrence was like an early emigrant who, seeing that his compatriots were ruined, or believed themselves ruined, went out to found a colony in an unexplored land. It is a mistake to think of him as an 'escapist' running away from Europe and trying to lose his unhappy modern consciousness in the dances of Mexican Indians. He was really occupied in discovering territories on which life could flourish and civilization shed its winding-sheet of what he called the 'cerebral consciousness'.

His search led him sometimes into absurdities, but this is unimportant compared with his criticism of the whole way of thinking of his contemporaries. What he attacked was the tendency, on the one hand, of the individualists to think of inner life as entirely determined by 'the present state of civilization', and on the other, that of the socialists to think of man as a social concept having certain potentialities and certain needs. He saw that the materialism of the socialists, the anti-materialism of the highly civilized 'intellectuals, although opposed in most respects, was one in sharing the cerebral concept of human individuality. And he wanted to connect individuality with life: physical life, unconscious life, and relations between human beings which had the force of primitive instinct. He wanted to disconnect human individuality from ideas about the position of the individual in relation to society. He wanted society to be changed but he wanted the change to be for the sake of man who was above society, not for the sake of society above man. He tried to express in literature what was almost inexpressible: a state of consciousness springing directly out of the most powerful and obscure forces where individuality becomes merged in the origins of life. In the course of the attempt he often got lost, and sometimes fell into traps—public and private ones, not the least of which was his own irritable and impatient personality.

His working-class origin was at once his greatest asset and that which made him sometimes escape from or leave unresolved important artistic and personal problems . . . Chiefly, an asset because the fact that he came from a social class different from that of most other writers meant that he was not born into their mental climate. He had the same kind of outside relation to his contemporaries as William Blake had to the other Romantics. Shelley attacked his world, but his ideas are vaporized in the intellectual attitudes of his time, which are those of a ruling class turning against itself, and therefore dependent too much on ideas. Blake brought to his attack the qualities of a man who possessed his own life and did not—in order to attack the aristocracy—have to dispossess himself. His criticism therefore has the added force of one who does not just use ideas but who speaks out of the wholeness of his own life: as much from his body as from his mind. Blake and Lawrence were not isolated intellectuals, they were outsiders, which is a more effective thing to be. And though Lawrence left his own people, he always remained at heart an outsider. His position is that of one who joins the upper class by attacking it—a Rape of the Sabine women. The characteristic situation in many of his stories is of gamekeeper, gardener, or gipsy who seizes on the aristocratic lady. And in the bourgeoisie, Lawrence thought of himself as an occupying power.

Thus the sense of his being outside without his losing a certain rootedness in his own origins always remained with him. Another attitude, springing out of his early experience and never lost, was the conviction that our physical well-being is an expression of our relationships with other people and even with nature. Lawrence's characters, in their relations with one another, are playing a game in which life and death are the stakes. Their meetings and separations are made intense by incipient resurrections, deaths, and murders. The following passage from *Women in Love* is characteristic of the way in which his dialogue is loaded with the ultimate consequences of psychological relationship. In this scene Birkin (who represents Lawrence himself) is making a copy of a Chinese drawing which he has found in the room of his hostess, Hermione Roddicce. Interrupted by Hermione, he describes the effect produced on him by the drawing, which is of geese:

> 'Why do you copy it?' she asked, casual and sing-song, 'Why not do something original?'
>
> 'I want to know it,' he replied. 'One gets more of China, copying this picture, than reading all the books.'
>
> 'And what do you get?'

She was at once roused, she laid as it were violent hands on him, to extract his secrets from him. She *must* know. It was a dreadful tyranny, an obsession in her, to know all he knew. For some time he was silent, hating to answer her. Then, compelled, he began:

'I know what centres they live from—what they perceive and feel—the hot bitter stinging heat of a goose's blood, entering their own blood like an inoculation of corruptive fire—fire of the cold-burning mud—the lotus mystery.'

Hermione looked at him along her narrow, pallid cheeks. Her eyes were strange and drugged, heavy under their heavy, drooping lids. Her thin bosom shrugged convulsively. He stared back at her, devilish and unchanging. With another strange, sick convulsion, she turned away, as if she were sick, could feel dissolution setting-in in her body. For with her mind she was unable to attend to his words, he caught her, as it were, beneath all her defences, and destroyed her with some insidious occult potency.

The lurid writing of such a passage may repel us, and yet it has the force of Lawrence's vision, that in their exchanges people are often in a relationship of murderer and murderee. It is as if Birkin and Hermione in this scene were, under their conversation, involved in a struggle necessary to each one's survival.

Such a view of life comes out of Lawrence's deepest experience, when in his childhood he was involved in a struggle of love and hate life-or-death with his mother. Of his mother's five children, Lawrence was her favourite son. His mother was a sensitive, perceptive woman, with aspirations towards gentility and a better class of life than that made possible by her marriage with Lawrence's father, a Nottinghamshire miner. She projected her frustrated hopes on to David Herbert—Bertie, as he was called—the youngest of her five children. She brought out in him all the delicacy, sensitivity, and compassion of his nature.

Lawrence's mother died in 1909, when he was twenty-four. Her death was so great a shock to him that he himself was nearly destroyed by it. We would know this from the poems he wrote and from *Sons and Lovers*, quite apart from the external confirmation which we have in the fact that in November 1911, a year later, he was affected in both lungs with tubercular pneumonia. That Lawrence felt his mother not only involved him in her death but wished him to die is clear from an unpublished document by

him which is in the library of the University of Cincinnati. Here
he sums up in a few sentences the background of his family:

> My mother fought with deadly hostility against my father, all her
> life. He was not hostile, till provoked, then he too was a devil. But
> my mother began it. She seemed to begrudge his very existence.
> She begrudged and hated her own love for him, she fought
> against his natural charm, vindictively. And by the time she died,
> at the age of fifty-five, she neither loved him nor hated him any
> more. She had got over her feeling for him, and was 'Free'. So
> she died of cancer.
>
> Her feeling for us, also, was divided. We were her own, there-
> fore she loved us. But we were his, so she despised us a little. I was
> the most delicate: a pale-faced, dirty-nosed frail boy. So she de-
> voted a great love to me. And she also despised me. I was one of
> the inferior brats her love for my father—or her disastrous marriage
> with him—had thrust upon her. She loved me tenderly. And for
> me, of course, she was the one being on earth: or so I *thought*,
> anyhow. But now, in the after-years, I realize that she had decided
> I was going to die, and that was a great deal to her.

Such a recollection, written four years before his death, surely
explains the attitude towards his characters contained in his letter
to Edward Garnett about *The Rainbow*:

> You mustn't look in my novel for the old stable ego of the char-
> acter. There is another ego, according to whose action the indi-
> vidual is unrecognizable, and passes through, as it were, allotropic
> states which it needs a deeper sense than any we've been used to
> exercise, to discover are states of the same radically-unchanged
> element. . . .

So Lawrence's outsideness was based on the very deeply experienced conviction that one is in a life-relationship with others
much deeper than 'character' talking to 'character'. This was
fortified by the memory, at least, of the class to which he belonged
which kept him an outsider from that he joined. In an essay called
Which Class I Belong To, also at the University of Cincinnati, he
writes, on returning from America:

> Here I am, nowhere, as it were, yet infinitely an outsider. And
> of my own choice.
>
> It is only this year, since coming back to Europe from America,

that I have asked myself why. Why, why, could I never go through the open door, into the other world? Why am I forever on the outskirts?

And it seems to me the answer is banal enough: class! I cannot go into the middle-class world. I have, as far as circumstances go, left the working-class world. So I have no world at all, and am content. . . .

What is the obstacle? I have looked for it in myself, as a clue to this dangerous cleavage between the classes. And I find it is a very deep obstacle. It is in the manner of contact. The contact, among the lower classes—as perhaps, in the past, among the aristocracy —is much more immediate, more physical between man and man, than ever it is among the middle classes. The middle class can be far more *intimate* yet never *so near* to one another. It is the difference between the animal, physical affinity that can govern the lives of men, and the other, the affinity of culture and purpose, which actually does govern the mass today.

But the affinity of culture and purpose that holds the vast middle-class world together seems to me to be an intensification, today, of the acquisitive and possessive instinct. The dominant instinct of the middle-class world, that is, of the whole world today, is the possessive instinct, which in its active form is the acquisitive instinct.

As an outsider, then, Lawrence attacked contemporary intellectual life which had got entangled inside its own ideas about its own situation. His starting point is outsideness, each person is outside everyone else and outside nature. It is on the basis of this separation of polarities that there is meeting between man and woman, people and 'birds, beasts and flowers'. If the sense of separateness is kept sacred, then meeting also becomes sacred, because it is like the vital touch of flint against steel. Out of a fusion of opposites, a spark is struck.

What Lawrence resists is the wrong kind of fusion, which consists in involvement with one another, the meeting in which people treat one another as physical property, or as mental idea. Meeting must be a fusion of polarities which are ultimately lonely and independent. Otherwise it leads to destruction, or to what he calls the cerebral attitude towards living.

If a meeting which is of polarities who are outside one another is impossible, then it is better to be alone than to become involved with others. So much emphasis has been laid on Lawrence and sex that it is important to emphasize his insistence on separateness of identity as the pre-condition of all creative relationships. Birkin puts the matter very clearly to Ursula in *Women in Love*:

'. . . At the very last, one is alone, beyond the influence of love. There is a real impersonal me, that is beyond love, beyond any emotional relationship. So it is with you. But we want to delude ourselves that love is the root. It isn't. It is only the branches. The root is beyond love, a naked kind of isolation, an isolated me, that does not meet and mingle, and never can.'

The characteristic Lawrence hero is Aaron, in *Aaron's Rod*, who is essentially alone and in search of a relationship in which he retains his aloneness. Lawrence's gamekeepers and gipsies are lonely, outside figures. Mellors, in *Lady Chatterley's Lover*, has refused to have anything to do with women for many years. The Australian part of *Kangaroo* is largely occupied with the efforts of Somers to get away from the possessive intellectual will of the politically conscious hero, Kangaroo.

Sex, then, is not an entry into a dark, lubricious, sticky 'inside' world, as Wyndham Lewis argues in his essay on Lawrence in *Paleface*. It is a meeting of opposite poles of existence, which, even in their meeting, retain their separateness, within a kind of blacking-out of consciousness, the entry of darkness like a third presence into the relationship . . . He attempts to describe it in *Fantasia of the Unconscious*:

We resolve back towards our elementals. We dissolve back, out of the upper consciousness, out of mind and sight and speech, back, down into the deep and massive, swaying consciousness of the dark, loving blood. At the last hour of sex I am no more than a powerful wave of mounting blood, which seeks to surge and join with the answering sea in the other individual. When the sea of individual blood which I am at that hour heaves and finds its pure contact with the sea of individual blood which is the woman at that hour, then each of us enters into the wholeness of our deeper infinitude, our profound fullness of being, in the ocean of our oneness and our unconsciousness.

Lest this seem to contradict what I have written about separateness, here is a further quotation from the same chapter:

> So it is in sex relation. There is a threefold result. First, the flash of pure sensation and real electricity. Then there is the birth of an entirely new state of blood in each partner. And then there is the liberation.

This perhaps seems hyperbole, until we let it take its place within Lawrence's whole attack on contemporary values. Lawrence attacks the idea that earning money should be the first aim of life, just as he attacks the concept of social man as a unit giving to society his potentiality and taking from it his need; and he attacks also the vision of doomed history within whose despair contemporary writers try to create for their own solace the mental patterns of their art.

In his insistence on sex Lawrence asserts a physical and instinctive value against dead machinery and cerebral ideas. He is appealing to the reality of the fact that we are both separate identities and yet all of one flesh, against a machine world and a shadow world. His insistence is so passionate that he makes the physical fact of sex more important even than love: because love, just as on the one side it is liable to become possessive, on the other it is liable to become too much mental concept.

However, it might also be said that in sex Lawrence is seeking for something beyond sex. It is remarkable that in all the studies written about him, no one has made the attempt to examine what is his idea of a perfect sexual relationship. Yet the attempt to define what he really meant by it is a central preoccupation of all the novels and many of the stories, from *The Rainbow* until *Lady Chatterley's Lover*, and it is further analysed in the two books about psycho-analysis, and several of the essays.

On the whole, Lawrence is better at saying what he thinks sex is not than what it is. The list is rather comical. It must not be mental or cerebral, it must not be Spanish, French, Italian, or Indian. It must not be enclosed by spiritual love. At times, like Rimbaud, he is on the verge of declaring a 'new love', which might even be homosexuality, but later he suggests that homosexuality is the 'sin against the Holy Ghost'. At times he seems to think that the ideal of love should be abolished from the sexual relation altogether. At other times, as in the story *Rawdon's Roof*, sex seems to be the compassion of the flesh between those who are bound together in love. Lawrence looks outside our civilization to Mexicans and Mexican Indians for a better sexual relationship, and to the past: to the Etruscans, the Florentines of the Renaissance, and the Greeks. He reproaches Jesus for not recognizing that which was sensual in the love of Mary Magdalene for him, and also in that of the Beloved Disciple, and even of Judas Iscariot. Almost at the end Lawrence tried to be most explicit and to describe the sexual act in a functional way. One feels that the pursuit was that of Tantalus and that the nearer he got to the goal of a definition, the more it evaded him.

His difficulty was that he did not want to make sex mental or cerebral, or even emotional. If we try to take away what was experimental, exasperated, and obsessive about his definitions, it surely amounts really to this. Sex, for him, is a confrontation of the whole passionate and sensual existence of one person by another. It concentrates a great many truths which acquire, through passion, the force to burn away hypocrisy, dirtiness, and shame. It is an admission, on the physical level, that our need for one another is greater than our need for many other things; and thus in its pride and humility it is an assertion of the value of human existence above materialism and intellectualism. It fuses within a moment the fierce joy of the satyrs and fauns, and the seriousness of the modern. So sex is really a symbolic act making channels through the falsity of modern civilization to human truth. Thus sex—or rather what Lawrence calls 'phallic consciousness'—leads beyond sex to a new relationship with the world outside one, and with oneself. At this point the label 'sex' can be taken away—as Lawrence did take it away at the end of his life; for if you have 'phallic consciousness', you may even do without sex. The point is to have a relationship with the world which consists of your own outsideness being in a state of lively awareness of the outsideness of other lives and other things.

However—leaving the question of his sexual 'obsession' aside, which so intrigues biographers like Aldington—one can see the

force of Lawrence's insistence on sex. It is the preacher's insistence
to his audience on a feeling for life, which, however much they
denied it, he could nail them down to. His 'obsession' with sex
is essentially an appeal to conscience. 'J'accuse,' he says in effect.
'You know that you are shifty, mean, ashamed, sniggering about
this thing. Or if you aren't that, you pretend to be above it. But
with your spiritual love, you starve and afflict your lovers and
pervert yourselves. Recognize this one fact about yourselves
which puts you in a brutally direct contact with another person.
Recognize that it is physical and instinctive and not just another
little high or low performance of your high or low mind. Do this
for the sake of one another, for the sake of that responsibility you
have to that in yourselves which is not yourselves: your body and
your instincts. If you do this one thing, submitting to what is
beyond yourselves, you may then with your conscious self demand forms of society which are for the sake of life. You may
put men on the pinnacle of the State instead of making the State
a pyramid entombing man.'

For sex, besides being the act, is thesis, antithesis, and synthesis.
Opposites, retaining each its separateness, merge, and out of this
fusion there is a new synthesis of living.

But Lawrence was not only a preacher. He was also a writer,
fighting a lonely battle against the whole contemporary tendency
of literature. That tendency was what he called the 'cerebral': the
tendency of writers like Rilke, Proust, Joyce, Eliot, to make
intellectual judgements about the condition of civilization in
their time, and then, within the situation so envisaged, to create
mental worlds of their own imagining which they sustained
within the larger world which was also their idea of the world.
An example of this way of creating a mental pattern within the
intellectually apprehended 'state of civilization' is contained in
the famous opening lines of T. S. Eliot's *The Love Song of
J. Alfred Prufrock*:

> Let us go then, you and I,
> When the evening is spread out against the sky
> Like a patient etherized upon a table;
> Let us go, through certain half-deserted streets,
> The muttering retreats

Of restless nights in one-night cheap hotels
And sawdust restaurants with oyster shells:
Streets that follow like a tedious argument
Of insidious intent
To lead you to an overwhelming question . . .

With Lawrence in mind, it may strike us that nothing could resemble a night sky less than a patient etherized upon a table. But the sky in Eliot's poem, although suggested by the sky over the roofs of a narrow street in a foggy town, is not the sky which contains stars hundreds of light-years distant from us. It is the sky of the mind of J. Alfred Prufrock, sensitive, intelligent, who has resigned all of his life except such visions as occasionally visit souls in hell.

The aim of Lawrence was to break out of this interior world into a place where outside objects are outside and real. His aim was like that which he attributes to Cézanne, when Cézanne painted an apple:

> After a fight tooth-and-nail for forty years, he did succeed in knowing an apple, fully; and, not quite as fully, a jug or two. That was all he achieved.
>
> It seems little, and he died embittered. But it is the first step that counts, and Cézanne's apple is a great deal more than Plato's idea. Cézanne's apple rolled the stone from the mouth of the tomb, and if poor Cézanne couldn't unwind himself from his cerements and mental winding-sheet, but had to lie still in the tomb, till he died, still he gave us a chance.

For Lawrence this apple stands for Cézanne's attempt to break out of the cerebral circle and get back in touch with the outsideness of nature . . . A jug or two also . . . Nothing could be less like the jugs, bridges, and so on of Rilke, which seek to enter the interior world of his mind in order to be named, and to become invisible.

And Lawrence's attitude is the exact opposite of that of a writer like Eliot. Eliot, in his poetry up to *The Hollow Men*, inhabits a world which is a mental view of the condition of civilization. When he looks at the sky he projects on to it an image of this world, as upon a lantern screen. Lawrence looks outside and tries to relate his own separate identity to the separate identity of sun and moon and stars. He sees himself as a three-dimensional object moving in space among other objects. He is filled with forces of instinctive life, as the sun has its fires. The problem confronting his intelligence is to move and attain equilibrium among other objects, relating oneself to them with forces of life deeper than the intelligence itself, as the spheres move in relation to oneself. To allow oneself, like Hamlet, to be dissuaded from this by thought, is to be imprisoned by intellect, instead of making use of it.

Lawrence's vision is just such a balancing of outer existences, which occasionally fuse when there is a meeting of the forces deeper than consciousness. His narratives are related in the form of a dialogue between the characters who are disguises of himself and those who are outside him, and nature which is also outside him. This relation is quivering and vital, it is like the flashing of light from object to object, and he brings to it a marvellous gift of mimicry, the power of imitating another without dissecting or turning the outside object inside out with analysis. His characters differ from those of other recent novelists not only in depicting the play of forces beneath personality, but also in the technique of imitation. His best dialogue has none of the qualities of interior monologue which attempts to express the idiom of thought. In a character as convincing as the young man in *The Fox*, the surface movements of the young man, his skin, his mouth, his eyes, seem as real as the iris-hued gloss on the neck-feathers of a pheasant. And in the poems of *Birds, Beasts and Flowers*, it is the wonderful gift for imitating in words external movement which convinces the reader of Lawrence's almost uncanny awareness of the instinctive life underneath this surface.

In his most ambitious early novel, *The Rainbow*, he paints an almost panoramic landscape which is a vision of the balancing harmony of external things, outside one another, and yet related by secret forces:

> Their life and interrelations were such; feeling the pulse and body of the soil, that opened to their furrow for the grain, and became smooth and supple after their ploughing, and clung to their feet with a weight that pulled with desire, lying hard and unresponsive when the crops were to be shorn away. The young corn waved

and was silken and the lustre slid along the limbs of the men who saw it. They took the udder of the cows, the cows yielded pulse and milk against the hands of the men, the pulse of the teats of the cows beat into the pulse of the hands of the men. They mounted their horses, and held life between the grip of their knees, they harnessed their horses at the wagon, and, with hand on the bridle-rings, drew the heaving of the horses after their will.

In autumn the partridges whirred up, birds in flocks blew like spray across the fallow, rooks appeared on the grey watery heavens and flew cawing into the winter. Then the men sat by the fire in the house where the women moved about with surety, and the limbs and the body of the men were impregnated with the day, cattle and earth and vegetation and the sky, the men sat by the fire and their brains were inert, as their blood flowed heavy with the accumulation from the living day.

A vision, I have pointed out, has wholeness and also a centre, because the wholeness radiates from the central focusing point. The essence of Lawrence's vision is polarities which are separate and yet related to one another by inner forces of instinctive life.

Nearly all the other writers I have discussed think of contemporary life as a state of civilization determined by contemporary history. They attempt to deal with this by creating worlds of values separate from the contemporary world, through their art. The peculiarity of Lawrence was that he denied altogether the existence of what one might term the threefold idea of contemporary necessity : the necessity which, like the Wilcoxes, you benefit by and support; the necessity which, like Mr. Prufrock, you recognize but do not accept; the necessity which, like Wells's heroes, you fight against with the social weapons of another necessity. Lawrence tried to cut through the present historic situation and appeal directly to the physical and spiritual being of each individual. He refused to accept ruling class materialism, but he also refused socialist materialism, and he rejected escapes into private cerebral worlds. He denied the concept of social man, and he regarded Wilcoxes, Prufrocks and the liberal or socialist heroes of Shaw, Wells and Galsworthy as being all 'social man'.

Lawrence could not accept any current attitudes. He wanted to break through all the theories of art and society, the entire structure of industrialism, and all the organizations of the Trades

Unionists, the methods of the revolutionaries, and the plans of the planners. All were equally repellent to him because all treated individual man as a function within society. It has been pointed out that he had fascist tendencies. All this means, however, is that occasionally he was deluded into accepting the talk of fascists about blood, race, and instinct. So soon as he saw that the fascists, like everyone else, were bureaucratic organizers, he lost sympathy for them.

He wanted to deal with life only in terms of nature, body, and instinct. He thought that if he could renew men's belief in these realities, they would perhaps change society for the sake of them. It is difficult, though, to see how the change could be made without mental calculations and submission to methods which would have been unsympathetic to him. Perhaps Lawrence's greatest weakness was a kind of impatience which was the result of an absolute refusal to face necessary ugliness. There is very little ugliness in any but his early work, and whenever he is faced by it he reacts with disgust and horror. He hated the places of his childhood and the life of the workers not just because he had grown away from them completely but because he could not endure the ugliness of the mining villages. And the hysteria in his work is not connected—as most critics think—with a sexual obsession but with a hatred which makes him want to run away from or destroy whatever ugliness he sees.

All the same, as a critic of contemporary life Lawrence is perhaps the greatest of this century, because he is the only one whose grasp of the values of living is never intellectualized or idealistic. It's always real. He tells us what we are are not and what we could be. He reminds us that we live among other human beings and that in our relationships we could be much realer than we are. He warns us against the danger of using our gifts, or following those who use their gifts, to create mental worlds of 'withinness' in the context of their fatalistic view of society. He has done more than any other writer to define the wholeness of individual existence, made up of body and instinct as well as intellect, and to show that this wholeness can be brought into relation with other people and the world outside.

Lawrence had social as well as individual passion, although he gave up as a bad job most of his attempts to save or to instruct society. But in one of his letters to Bertrand Russell written during the First World War he writes, referring to E. M. Forster: 'His ultimate desire is for the continued action which has been called the social passion—the love for humanity—the desire to work for humanity. That is every man's ultimate desire and need.' And although Lawrence's attempts to get together with Bertrand Russell and save the world were foredoomed and absurd, the social passion ultimately exists and is real in his writing. Lawrence's work holds out the feasible light of a kind of society where life is lived for the sake of the concrete realities of human separateness and human relations.

VI

HAMMERED GOLD AND GOLD
ENAMELLING OF HUMANITY

YEATS was a humanist in the manner of his own idea of the Italian Renaissance, which he got from Pater and Symons, not at all in that of, say, T. H. Huxley. For him the Renaissance was a link between Italy and the Greece of Greek tragedy, where the tragic chorus danced in frenzied joy over the corpses of the dead. Art must bring to perfection the form of joy which emerged from tragic life, whose function was to be rejected and die. For him individuality was justified not by the individual himself, the person, but by his capacity to produce what was impersonal, perhaps an example of the ritual of living, perhaps a heroic act, perhaps a work of art. Like Rilke, Yeats is a poet of transcendence, but the direction in which experiences are transcended is, as it were, reversed. For Rilke outside objects are transformed into invisible inner life where they become part of the human whole. For Yeats inner life is transformed into external objects, artefacts, which represent the triumph of the spirit over the torment of living. Life streams upwards from shapeless subjectivity into formative dream:

> Death and life were not
> Till man made up the whole,
> Made lock, stock and barrel
> Out of his bitter soul,
> Aye, sun and moon and star, all.
> And further add to that
> That, being dead, we rise,
> Dream, and so create
> Translunar Paradise.

In the poem called 'Sailing to Byzantium', the first in *The Tower*, which was written at the height of his achievement, he aspires to an eternal existence as a work of art:

> Once out of nature I shall never take
> My bodily form from any natural thing,
> But such a form as Grecian goldsmiths make
> Of hammered gold and gold enamelling
> To keep a drowsy emperor awake;
> Or set upon a golden bough to sing.

In a second poem on the same theme (Byzantium represents in his poetry that civilization where every artisan was a philosopher) he expresses the idea that the created object is the apex where the human becomes more than human:

> A starlit or a moonlit dome disdains
> All that man is,
> All mere complexities,
> The fury and the mire of human veins.

and:

> I hail the superhuman;
> I call it death-in-life and life-in-death . . .

The idea at first sight seems to resemble Rilke's thought in the *Duino Elegies*, that boundaries between living and being dead are too sharply defined, and that in the Whole both phases of existence freely mingle. But death, for Rilke, is a sublimated intensity of life, projected into the minds of those who are living, by saints, lovers, and heroes. Rilke regards the dead as belonging to an invisible world of the mind where they are wooed back among mundane things. But Yeats regards death as the transformation of life into a superhuman pattern of living.

With the symbolism of the angels, Rilke externalizes his subjectivity by projecting what, until then, had been his own isolated poet's task, into the world. We might almost think the angels illustrate his awareness that he is no longer alone in his poetry. But the angels are superhuman only in their powers. Their function is simply to bring visible and invisible together, not to turn them into the supernatural.

In Yeats's thought, the greatness of the achievement of the creative will is to sacrifice tragic life on altars where the pure gold of idea or art or ritual is purged of the dross of actual living and becomes transformed, symbolic, artificial life. In order to do this and to justify it, a whole system of supernatural machinery is evoked. In a sense, Yeats is serious (or means to be) when he declares that when he has left the human shape his soul will assume some predestined artificial pattern. And yet, although we are sometimes convinced of his seriousness, he gives us less feeling of the supernatural than several who insist less on it: than Rimbaud or Eliot, or even than Lawrence when Lawrence writes his *Ship of Death*.

Where Yeats does convince us, and where he seems greater than Rilke, is in his acceptance of the necessity of sacrifice in order that man may create the monuments of his own greatness. Rilke never rises above the tendency to regard poetry as communication of interior with exterior world; he never escapes entirely from his preoccupation with the problems of personal existence even when he has projected the personal into impersonal symbol. He sees man isolated in his universe among things which continue and animals who are unaware of death; he wants poetry to give the earth invisible inner spiritual significance, while at the same time giving human existence the assurance and continuity of things, animals and spiritual intensity. The magnificence of Yeats lies in his regarding existence only as a means to create transcendent objects which are a higher existence, a life concretized in death. The sacrifice involved, and all the pathos and suffering of man in the process, do not bother him. Joy lies in the achievement of superhuman art, and the corpses at the base of the monuments can be trampled down in the triumphant dance. To Rilke poetry is a flow of one thing into another, visible into invisible. To Yeats it is crystallization of certain patterns of experience into objects which are superhuman.

Nor does Yeats use poetry to create an interior world of value salvaged from the past. He is suspicious of intellectualization, as also of emotions which turn inwards. In the Introduction to *The Oxford Book of Modern Verse*, he justifies his rejection of the war poems of Wilfred Owen and Siegfried Sassoon thus:

In poems that had for a considerable time fame, written in the first person, [these writers] made that suffering their own. I have rejected these poems for the same reason that made Arnold withdraw his *Empedocles on Etna* from circulation; passive suffering is not a theme for poetry. In all the great tragedies, tragedy is a joy to the man who dies; in Greece the tragic chorus danced. When man has withdrawn into the quicksilver at the back of the mirror no great event becomes luminous in his mind; it is no longer possible to write *The Persians, Agincourt, Chevy Chase*: some blunderer has driven his car on the wrong side of the road—that is all.

If one admires Owen, one may quarrel with this. However, what I am concerned with here is the phrase 'the quicksilver at the back of the mirror'. Yeats wanted to have in his work outside relationships with objects outside himself. He rejected both the intellectual and the emotional self-regarding inner world. Here his aristocratic sense of 'contact' between men without destructive intimacy seems to join forces with what Lawrence felt about the miners.

In several respects the parallel of the Irish aristocratic Yeats with the Nottinghamshire miner Lawrence is striking. Both divided humanity into the insensate, unawake mass and the 'lords of life'. Both understood some value of the intuition of the blood which they set above the knowledge of the intellectuals. Both looked back across the gulf of Christianity to a pre-Christian pagan era, where they imagined men to have natural wisdom. The dance, above all the pagan dance, was sacred to both. Towards the end of his life, Yeats developed an attitude towards sex which was akin to that of Lawrence, and perhaps even he may have understood the the significance of Lawrence. At all events, his selection of Lawrence's poems in the Oxford book shows a sympathy which he did not feel for certain other modern poets. Both felt a dithyrambic urge to destroy existing civilization rather than accept it on the terms of misery, self-pity and intellectualization. This resemblance—and also the difference between Yeats and Lawrence—may be illustrated by two quotations. In a poem called 'Lapis Lazuli', from *Last Poems*, Yeats has these lines:

> . . . For everybody knows or else should know
> That if nothing drastic is done
> Aeroplane and Zeppelin will come out,

Pitch like King Billy bomb-balls in
Until the town lie beaten flat.

All perform their tragic play,
There struts Hamlet, there is Lear,
That's Ophelia, that Cordelia;
Yet they, should the last scene be there,
The great stage curtain about to drop,
If worthy their prominent part in the play,
Do not break up their lines to weep.
They know that Hamlet and Lear are gay;
Gaiety transfiguring all that dread.
All men have aimed at, found and lost;
Black out; Heaven blazing into the head:
Tragedy wrought to its uttermost.

In *The Triumph of the Machine* Lawrence contemplates the same universal ultimate disaster:

So mechanical man in triumph seated upon the seat of his machine
will be driven mad from himself, and sightless, and on that day
the machines will turn to run into one another
traffic will tangle up in a long-drawn-out crash of collision
and engines will rush at the solid houses; the edifice of our life
will rock in the shock of the mad machine, and the house will come
     down.
Then, far beyond the ruin, in the far, the ultimate, remote places
the swan will lift up again his flattened, smitten head
and look round, and rise, and on the great vaults of his wings
will sweep round and up to greet the sun with a silky glitter of a new
     day
and the lark will follow trilling, angerless again,
and the lambs will bite off the heads of the daisies for friskiness.
But over the middle of the earth will be the smoky ruin of iron
the triumph of the machine.

Both accept, even with gaiety, the destruction of civilization. Both foresee that if man is doomed, by the short-circuit of his machinery and his ideology, then life will re-emerge in some other form. Although Yeats's poem contains his cyclic view of history (All things fall and are built again, / And those that build them again are gay) it is not this which really impresses us. What is striking in the poem is Yeats's idea of the aesthetic gesture as vindication of tragedy, and as a symptom of the emergence of life-within-death and death-within-life, which is gay. With Lawrence, what takes the place of the destroyed civilization is wild nature, and where Lawrence would quarrel with Yeats would be in setting 'life' above art.

The centre of Yeats's vision is an aesthetic object: stone, tragic gesture, poem, statue. The purpose of all his supernatural machinery is to externalize this symbol, to give it a reality outside the poetry, outside the interior of his own mind. The subjective creative will has to know that it can create something which is not just a reflection of its own isolation, not just a household god in the shadowy cave of the poet's own mind. It has to place what it creates in a past and future where men's minds are not turned inwards like the quicksilver at the back of the glass.

What distinguishes Yeats from the Symbolists and post-Symbolists is the effort he made to give external authority to his symbols. The Symbolists, and Rilke, are content for the most part to translate their experiences into terms of their own inner life and create symbols which the reader can only understand by entering their closed-in intellectual spheres. Yeats is consumed by a passion to project his metaphors into an external framework which supports and affirms them, giving them as it were a life or super-life of their own, outside his own subjectivity. In his autobiographies we watch the evolution of a whole vocabulary and an extensive programme of action, whereby he projects himself into his 'opposite' which is at once impersonal and a higher form of individual existence.

The idea of 'the mask' which plays so much part in his work—and one can truly also say in his life—is of external gesture, form, or pose in which the projected interior self meets and indeed fuses with the outside world. Yeats's biographer Richard Ellmann indicates several stages of development in the concept of the mask. In its simplest meaning, he tells us, 'the mask is the social self'. But it is also that disguise (or self-projection) with which we confront both 'the world and the beloved'. In a sense it is the truest self, because it is the form assumed by that essence of our

personalities which others think us. Thus Rilke's saints and frustrated lovers with their intensity of concentrated existence correspond to what Yeats meant by the mask .The mask is also
'defensive armour'; and it is, too, a weapon of attack, an idealized
conception of ourselves with which we can go into battle.

Perhaps the most important thing to note about Yeats's concepts is that they are not the interior categories of a man living in
his own shut-off mental world. They are organic, and they are
supposed to be external. For example, the mask is organic because
it develops out of Yeats's own life, out of the simplest and most
complex needs; the simple need of a very shy man to put on a
face with which to meet other people, and the far more complex
need of externalizing the art of a man particularly isolated in his
circumstances. When one looks into ideas like 'mask', 'anti-self',
and 'opposite' in Yeats, more and more they seem slogans in a
struggle he was undertaking with his time. A struggle to break
through the incense and mists of the Aesthetic Movement and the
Celtic Twilight, to avoid the subjective extremes of the Symbolists, to refuse the proud temptations of an exalted, scholarly
intellectualism, to be drawn into and yet withdraw from the
activities of the Irish nationalists and to attack the scientific views
of Tyndal and Huxley.

Yeats not only invented private categories to which he attributed
an objective purpose, but he also attended séances and joined
movements and causes, all to the same purpose: of finding confirmation in outside things of his own inner world. To anyone
except him the Irish Myth would have meant one of two things:
either becoming a poet in the folk tradition, like Padraic Colum
or James Stephens, or weaving one obscure strand into an immense intellectual pattern composed of thousands of such strands,
as it did with James Joyce. But for Yeats the myth provided one
more outlet from his subjective preoccupations, one more experiment in getting away from the stifling aestheticism of the Rossetti
circle of his father's friends, and getting his poetry on to the road
of real people and outside things.

And the true appeal of every movement he joined is really that
it was external. Nationalism, and the committees he started, and
the editing, and the theatre-managing and play-producing and

play-writing, all brought him out of his interior world among the outside things.

His spiritualism may seem to contradict this, but it does not really do so. For in Yeats's accounts of his table rappings, the things he saw, the sounds he heard, the smells he smelled, and even the dreams he dreamed, he is concerned with proving two things: that they came from the outside, and that others had the same experiences too. This preoccupation never leaves him. In 'Hodos Chameliontos,' the section of *The Trembling of the Veil* where he describes his summers passed at Rosses Point with his uncle, George Pollexfen, what he wants to show is that his uncle and himself became aware at the same time of the same cabbalistic symbols.

> There are some high sand-hills and low cliffs, and I adopted the practice of walking by the seashore while he walked on cliff or sand-hill; I, without speaking, would imagine the symbol, and he would notice what passed before his mind's eye, and in a short time he would practically never fail of the appropriate vision. .

In the preface to *A Vision* he insists that the whole system of the book was dictated to him by unknown spirit writers, through the mediumship of his wife. He does not tell us this in order to make the incredible seem more credible by a show of confirmatory evidence. Indeed, he hedges whenever the question of whether he 'believes' in his visions crops up. What he does wish to demonstrate is that they are not subjective fantasies. When he uses magic, like Rimbaud, he is being dictated to by objective forces, and even hallucinations come from the outside. Although —perhaps because he is too 'civilized'—he does not give us the 'overwhelming conviction of the supernatural', he does, like Rimbaud, make us believe that the visions he sees somehow come from an objective world and are not just a private madness.

★   ★   ★   ★

The Introduction to *The Oxford Book of Modern Verse* is irritating because it says little that justifies Yeats as an editor qualified to select the work of contemporaries. Yet it is revealing about Yeats himself and his relation to his contemporaries.

What he says, for example, about Eliot and Pound is far more interesting as a revelation of his own aims—the opposite of what he rejects in theirs—than valuable as criticism. Of Eliot he writes that 'he has described men and women that get out of bed or into it from mere habit; in describing life that has lost heart his own art seems grey, cold, dry'. In *The Waste Land* he discovers that 'amid much that is moving in symbol and imagery there is much monotony of accent'. Of Ezra Pound he writes:

> When I consider his work as a whole I find more style than form; at moments more style, more deliberate nobility and the means to convey it than in any contemporary poet to me, but it is constantly interrupted, broken, twisted into nothing by its direct opposite, nervous obsession, nightmare, stammering confusion; he is an economist, poet, politician, raging at malignants with inexplicable characters and motives, grotesque figures out of a child's book of beasts. . . . Style and its opposite can alternate, but form must be full, sphere-like, single.

'The monotony of accent' he discovers in Eliot is surely the greyness of an interior world whose circumference is the mechanic habit of modern life. But in writing of the poems of Dorothy Wellesley he expresses his own deepest views about poetry:

> The individual soul, the betrayal of the unconceived at birth, are among her themes, it must go further still, must become its own betrayer, its own deliverer, the one activity, the mirror turn lamp.

The excitement here makes the utterance clouded. But the drift is clear. What agitates him is the idea of the soul becoming symbol, poem, lamp. And returning later in the Introduction to her poetry—and throwing three other poets into the discussion—he exclaims: 'Here stands not this or that man but man's naked mind.'

This throws as much light on Yeats himself as obscurity on the poets being discussed. In these other poets he recognizes his own struggle, through his concepts, to externalize inward dream or thought by means of the 'opposite' or the 'mask'. But the image or symbol so created is not just the representation of the inward dream. It is a transformation of the inner into some phase of objective life in the external system of a superhuman world where the symbolic is the real. So the 'one activity, the mirror turned lamp' is the life-in-death and death-in-life where the creative mind becomes one with the symbol created.

The central theme of his later poetry is the transformation of the creative imagination into the thing created, its opposite, which —though defiantly artificial and impersonal and inhuman—is also part of the pattern of a superhuman existence. This process— I repeat—is not confined to the world of the poet's own imagination. Once it has left his separate inner mind and become the 'opposite', then it supposedly enters into the external system which has been 'dictated' to him, and set down in his book *A Vision*.

As many critics have pointed out, the reader cannot believe in Yeats's mythology. What does one mean here by not believing? Well, for one thing, one does not believe in *A Vision*. Yeats himself does not appear to believe in it very much, for that matter; nor even the spirits who dictated it to him, who explain that all they are doing is providing him with metaphors for his poetry. Indeed, in some of his poems the references to *A Vision* affect us much as pieces of scaffolding do when they are left on buildings. One feels the building would be better without them.

All the same, there is something about Yeats's beliefs which does convince us. This is the sense of the monumental nature of man's aims when they are directed towards art, idea, passion, gesture, or cause. He does make us see that man creates something more important than man, something which disdains its creator, and that this art-object is yet profoundly human—in fact is perhaps the true humanity, and all the rest sentiment and self-pity.

Where he seems to meet with Shakespeare at certain points of feeling and thought is in his capacity to reach, without ever crossing, a borderline beyond which the aim of man to rise above his human weakness and create an image of his own greatness becomes inhuman. He seems, indeed, to define exactly the place where the personal can meet with the impersonal, and the human with the superhuman, the self with the anti-self, without losing humanity. In doing this he enlarges our concept of humanity and

criticizes current ideas based on feelings of pity or despair about
the contemporary 'human situation'.

Yeats's sense of the highest human aims has none of the brutal
self-assertiveness of Nietzsche's Superman, nor the intellectual
hygienic coldness of Shaw, nor the stony perfectionism of Stefan
George. In telling us that we are less important than what we can
make as dome, stone, gold, gesture, or ritual of living, he is telling
us something about ourselves. His iciest and most exalted images
are fused with the creative passion of man.

His theme is the transformation of imperfect and subjective man
into his objective aims. A clear example of this is already implicit
in the beautiful poem 'Easter 1916', in which the symbolism of
the word 'stone' is used with a double effect.

> Hearts with one purpose alone
> Through summer and winter seem
> Enchanted to a stone
> To trouble the living stream.
> The horse that comes from the road,
> The rider, the birds that range
> From cloud to tumbling cloud,
> Minute by minute they change;
> A shadow of cloud on the stream
> Changes minute by minute;
> A horse-hoof slides on the brim,
> And a horse plashes within it;
> The long-legged moor-hens dive,
> And hens to moor-cocks call;
> Minute by minute they live:
> The stone's in the midst of all.

The stone here symbolizes the 'terrible beauty' of those who
are born by their deaths into human greatness. Abruptly, in
the lines immediately following those quoted above, the significance of the word 'stone' is reversed, with an effect almost of
thoughtlessness:

> Too long a sacrifice
> Can make a stone of the heart.
> O when may it suffice?
> That is Heaven's part, our part

> To murmur name upon name,
> As a mother names her child
> When sleep at last has come
> On limbs that had run wild.
> What is it but nightfall?
> No, no, not night but death;
> Was it needless death after all?

So one theme of the Irish martyrs of the Easter Rising is divided between two tides of feeling, and each is bounded, as it were, by the symbol of the stone. The one tide is a meditation on the turbulent, uneven, achieved lives of these men and women who have suddenly attained the immortality of martyrs. A profound uneasiness like a stirring under deep waters culminates in the bitter exclamation: 'Too long a sacrifice / Can make a stone of the heart.' Viewed, as Rilke might say, from the side of life, the poet cannot completely accept either the lives or the deaths of his friends. And his suspicion of the cause for which they have sacrificed themselves concretizes in the image of the heart of stone, from which all human sensibility has been drained. (Throughout the poem we feel that Yeats grieves over the insufficient attention that his friends had paid to their lives.) But the tide which flows in the opposite direction, from the side of death, marvels at the 'terrible beauty' made by the deaths of these patriots. The stone symbolizes what is eternal and monumental in their death, where they have been 'transformed utterly' from what they were into 'terrible beauty'.

'The withered stone of the heart' on the one hand, and on the other the stone which is the transformation of life into beauty, are two opposites which represent a conflict in Yeats's own mind between the cause which justified the sacrifice of personal living to it and that which withers the heart of all personal feeling. And between the two he was never, before his fiftieth year, drawn deeply into what most people regard as life. As a young man he thought, like the hero of *Axel's Castle*, that life should be lived for the aristocrats of life by their servants, and he had created a religion of his own imaginings, having the dogma: 'Because those imaginary people are created out of the deepest instinct of man, to be his measure and his norm, whatever I can imagine those mouths speaking may be the nearest I can go to truth.'

The reader of his *Autobiography* is struck by Yeats's detachment from life. He feels himself outside the lives of his fellow-poets in London, the members of a 'tragic generation'. He does not judge them harshly for their various forms of dissipation. At bottom what he is always asking is whether drunkenness and debauchery help Beardsley, Lionel Johnson, Symons, and Wilde in their art. He has little life of his own, except his occult inquiries and his reading, being disqualified from any fulfilment of his feelings by his frustrated passion for Maud Gonne.

However, if the Tragic Generation of the Rhymers' Club represents a kind of Scylla which Yeats, with his senses sealed by frustrated passion, easily steers past, there is also Charybdis, more difficult to avoid, and that is the lives of his patriotic Irish friends, including Maud Gonne herself, absorbed as they were in the fanaticism of their cause.

His tottering, scholarly rhymster friends were all too human, and his fanatical Irish friends had substituted a cause for the cultivation of their humanity. Reading between the lines of J. B. Yeats's letters to him, it is clear that his father thought Yeats himself was in danger of becoming dehumanized.

The central interest of his autobiography and his autobiographical poetry is that in the course of his development he became more rather than less human. His humanity shows how much critical intelligence he combined with his creativeness, for few men can have been offered so many excuses for freezing into attitudes of coldness, bitterness, intellectual superiority, public manners, political fanaticism, or other-worldly mysticism. The drama of his life is the parade of all these attractive and honourable possibilities before his eyes, and his refusal to be taken in by them.

The humanity he evolved, however, was not the easy-going, sentimental kind which enables most of us to call ourselves human. To be human seems the most facile of our attainments. For Yeats it was the most difficult. His humanity was of that temperature where the greatest cold burns like the hottest fire. It is when he ascends in his poetry to the mountain tops where everything seems snow that we are most aware of his human warmth. It is

the humanity resolved out of contempt for mere human existence,
of his portrait of 'The Fisherman':

> The living men that I hate,
> The dead man that I loved,
> The craven man in his seat,
> The insolent unreproved,
> And no knave brought to book
> Who has won a drunken cheer,
> The witty man and his joke
> Aimed at the commonest ear,
> The clever man who cries
> The catch-cries of the clown,
> The beating down of the wise
> And great Art beaten down.
>
> Maybe a twelvemonth since
> Suddenly I began,
> In scorn of this audience,
> Imagining a man,
> And his sun-freckled face
> And grey Connemara cloth,
> Climbing up to a place
> Where stone is dark under froth,
> And the down-turn of his wrist
> When the flies drop in the stream;
> A man who does not exist,
> A man who is but a dream;
> And cried, 'Before I am old
> I shall have written him one
> Poem maybe as cold
> And passionate as the dawn'.

It is derived, too, from mourning over those whom he has seen
sacrifice their humanity to some bitter feeling or public cause. In
'Prayer for my Daughter' he exorcizes the hatred that makes a
'stone of the heart':

> An intellectual hatred is the worst,
> So let her think opinions are accursed.
> Have I not seen the loveliest woman born
> Out of the mouth of Plenty's horn,

> Because of her opinionated mind
> Barter that horn and every good
> By quiet natures understood
> For an old bellows full of angry wind?

His humanity does not spring just out of his creative-critical intelligence. It also comes from a quality of his own personality which one notes particularly in comments on other men. This was a certain magnanimity, a largeness of soul which includes within its generality whatever particular situation he is describing. In his writing we always feel the presence of a spirit which is beyond the particular object, however intense his absorption in the particular. This is perhaps why, on the one hand, he gives us no conviction of the supernatural however much he appears to believe in it, and why, on the other, this incredibility of his demons, witches, Michael Robartes, Lunar Phases, and the rest does not really bother us. We accept it partly as structural device, and partly we are captivated by the quality of his mind which is always beyond the particular assertion. When in his memoirs, or in a poem like 'All Souls Night', he writes of his friends, apparently trivial anecdotes are made significant by the personal legend which encloses them. Out of anecdotes and myths he creates his own myth, which, at the end, seems divided between Lear and the fool.

His magnanimity also suggests something beyond himself: that he and those whose memories he lingers over are contained within a larger collective consciousness, a mind of all humanity.

The centre of Yeats's vision is the stone amid the whirling stream, the artefact into which experience is projected where it acquires transformed existence after it has been purged of mere life. Mask, opposite, and artefact, however, also exist within the circumference of larger magnanimity which is the whole sum of his thinking projected into the system of categories described in *A Vision*.

This extraordinary volume is a stumbling-block to Yeats admirers. It opens with a section called *A Packet For Ezra Pound*. This is part letter, part journal, and contains the Rimbaudesque claim: 'I send you the introduction of a book which will, when finished, proclaim a new divinity.' Next there follows *Stories of*

Michael Robartes and His Friends—an attempt to provide a mythical framework for the system. Only after these bewildering preludes do we arrive at the main matter—itself ushered in with references to Empedocles, and Simplicius, followed by Alcemon (a pupil of Pythagoras), Heraclitus, Dr. Dee, Macrobius, Dr. Sturm, and Swedenborg. There are also geometric cones, diagrams, and tables which illustrate the categories of human characters and lunar phases.

One of the most remarkable features of *A Vision* is that Yeats's system, which divides the history of civilizations into twenty-three lunar phases, also describes human individuals in terms of the same categories. For instance, an individual can belong to the phase (the fifteenth) which is most subjective, and so can a historic epoch. It might seem that there was contradiction here, because surely if a period of history enters a phase when all things revert to their beginnings, or which is the highest point in that civilization, then men also should belong to that phase. On second thoughts, however, Yeats's system makes allowance for and even provides a hypothesis for explaining the fact that certain individuals do not seem to belong to the period of history into which they are born. They are anachronisms unable to influence that period which robs them of the means of fulfilling their destinies.

If Yeats's system is regarded as a metaphor, then it becomes interesting, because like his later poems it does provide a framework for a criticism of historic events and individual lives. According to *A Vision*, contemporary civilization in 1927 entered the twenty-third phase of the moon when it moves into the darkness of what he calls 'objectivity'. (Historically speaking he thinks of an objective phase as one in which the subjective individuality of men is driven out by dogmatism and conformity.) Here all individuality is submerged under the colourless anonymity of the masses. The aim of everyone is to behave like everyone else and all expressions of subjective originality are regarded as subversive. By contrast, the fifteenth phase is 'full moon', when 'subjectivity' is at its most brilliant development. In terms of our civilization this means the period of the Italian Renaissance.

Regarded in this way as metaphor, the system of *A Vision* dramatizes Yeats's own vision of what is happening to civilization.

It also shows that he believes that the fate of civilization is assumed into a larger mind of humanity, which knows no end. The wheel revolves and the point where contemporary man is situated in it is sometimes in darkness, sometimes in light.

The direction of Yeats's vision of humanity is a vertical one. The movement of tragic human fate is a going up and a going down. Life itself is trampled under the earth, but the individual who accepts the destruction of his life, and concentrates on making the object which is mask or anti-self, then becomes through that very object part of the pattern of 'life-in-death and death-in-life'. What is true of the individual is also true of humanity. A generation is destroyed, but in the forms of thought or art which it has created, it is assumed into the pattern of a world mind. This metaphor might be barbaric or brutal or coldly abstract. But it is not. Yeats succeeds in identifying the noblest human achievements with a higher form of existence which remains human. Achievements of intellect, art, and passion are worth the sacrifice of living they involve, because they take their place in a pattern of all life.

VII

ANTI-VISION AND DESPAIR

THE subject-matter of visionary writers, even when it is the present, has a kind of bias towards the future. Poets like Rimbaud in *Les Illuminations*, Yeats in *A Second Coming*, and Eliot in *The Waste Land* have their insights into the present, but if their apocalyptic visions referred only to the present, these would seem exaggerated. The exaggeration is that part of the work which is directed towards the future. To a lesser degree Forster, when he writes about the parting of Aziz and Fielding at the end of *A Passage to India*, and Lawrence in all he has to say about instinctual relationships, show concern with the future. Indirectly they are saying: 'If you neglect these personal relations, then . . .' With Forster, the 'then' is followed by silence as far as his novel-writing is concerned.

Prophetic warning is justified in our time more perhaps than in others by the dramatic conflict of potentialities in our world. One description of our period might be The Age with Two Futures. Everything that is potentiality in us has a double destructive and creative aspect. There has never been an age in which communities and individuals had a greater possibility of developing towards greater happiness and freedom. Yet at the same time, we feel a tomorrow pressing upon us which may bring the destruction of individuality, and perhaps also of all our civilization. The one quality these futures have in common is that both are materialistic. Visions and anti-visions are today based on interest in material potentialities. Renunciation of interest in the material development or destruction of our world means renunciation of the individualist vision. And the orthodox writers—or those in search of orthodoxy—are those least concerned about the world's future.

The individualist visionary has contemplated the transcendence of the conditions of modern life into an unprecedented liberation of the human spirit, or conversely, unprecedented destruction of everything, including the spirit. *Les Illuminations* and *Une Saison en Enfer*: Vision and Anti-Vision. Beyond anti-vision there lies that renunciation of interest in the material future which is our modern form of orthodoxy.

Nearly a quarter of a century divides the publication of two works which, between them, span the whole anti-vision. One is *The Waste Land*; and the other *1984*.

There are deeper divisions between these two works than that one is a poem and the other a novel, one an accepted masterpiece, the other still something less than this. They deal, really, with quite different worlds, though they add up to one world. Eliot is primarily concerned with the collapse of cultural and religious values amid a scene which is the breakdown of the material structure of civilization. Although there is a feeling of crowds and of neurotic situations in his poem, there is little feeling for 'the people', the 'proles' of Orwell's novel. People are just part of the scenery in what is a tragedy of an almost impersonal civilized consciousness self-aware through poetic sensibility. The scene drawn from contemporary life in *The Waste Land*—the 'pub' scene at the end of 'A Game of Chess'—contains the only lines in which the vitality of the poetry seems to fail and the inspiration to become mechanical.

Although *The Waste Land* contains a vision of the whole history of the West falling into ruin, it is a vision of a disaster without any historic cause. In some of the most beautiful lines of the poem the collapse of the West is compared with the shipwreck in *The Tempest* which flings Ferdinand, 'Musing upon the king my brother's wreck / And on the king my father's death before him', upon the island. There is no conflict of historic development. The whole of history is viewed, through the present, as one scene of disaster. This above all produces a feeling of the irremediable hopeless helplessness of all the situations within the poem. Within history, no force can save history, and the only hope which might possibly come would be from outside ('O Lord, Thou pluckest me out').

The poem's concentrated power is largely due to this view of history as a cosmic disaster, comparable to a shipwreck or earthquake. The reader's sympathies are not engaged in a struggle for good against evil, or in any awareness of hope. The result of this lack of concern with historic causes is to intensify the feelings of religious, moral, and aesthetic disaster, which are, as it were, purified of connection with history. The collapse of civilization appears simply as the collapse of values and achievements whose loss is visualized and echoed in a kind of hollow emptiness. There is no indication whether Eliot feels the moral condition and the neurosis glimpsed in one or two scenes to be the cause of the disaster or the disaster to be the cause of this decay. The sensibility which depicts and mourns is of the mind of a whole civilization which is both victim and witness of its own dereliction. This mind is to some extent also—in its fragmentariness and unconnectedness—itself an object and product of the external disaster. Consciousness has become scattered and fragmented. Its unanswered question is not whether the ruins which are its body can be repaired but whether the soul can be saved from the ruins. If there is any hope in the poem it is the hope that the soul may be separated and rescued from the irremediably ruined civilization.

There are certain parallels between Eliot's and Orwell's despair, though no meeting place. One parallel is that in the poetry written before *The Waste Land* (and also in *The Waste Land* itself) there are glimpses of a civilization which is not anti-vision, a Golden Age submerged under the confusion of the present, like a Greek bronze among rubbish—the vision which is the anti-vision's opposite. The idea of a positive good condition compared with which the anti-vision is *disappointment* is more strongly felt in Orwell. It never entirely loses its bitter force and is the positive clue to the negative world of *1984*. With Eliot the vision is simply the glimpse of a world where there were once positive values amid the reality of the present. The most characteristic of all Eliot's effects is his habit of placing lines describing the squalor of the modern against those evoking the coherent greatness of the past: vision set directly against anti-vision. The effect is architectural: as though a line of Renaissance buildings were divided only by a single narrow lane from a line of slums:

But where is the penny world I bought
    To eat with Pipit behind the screen?
The red-eyed scavengers are weeping
    From Kentish Town and Golder's Green;

Where are the eagles and the trumpets?

    Buried beneath some snow-deep Alps.
Over buttered scones and crumpets
    Weeping, weeping multitudes
Droop in a hundred A.B.C.'s.

Under the irony there is the glimpse of established order of past civilization bursting through the present, as through flimsy.

The greatness of *The Waste Land* is in Eliot's realization that his kind of modern poetic consciousness is involved in and conditioned by the state of civilization. He abandons here the position of Prufrock, which is really the same as that of the *Three Sisters* or *Mrs. Dalloway* : the position of one whose sensibility sets him outside and above his circumstances, and whose vision of what has been lost becomes more significant than the thing lost itself. The mermaids who do not sing to Prufrock are realer than any that could sing.

*   *   *   *

In Orwell's *1984* negative anti-vision is also measured against positive vision, but the nature of the vision is, of course, quite different. Orwell writes as completely out of social consciousness as Eliot does out of a feeling for the greatness of the past. Like Eliot's despair, Orwell's is measured against a gauge of what is lost—or, rather, with him, of what might have been found. The clue to the disappointment is contained in the very remarkable essay (supposedly a chapter from the book written by Goldstein about the history of Eurasia) which forms the centre of *1984*.

In this chapter of a book within the novel, Goldstein analyses the events which supposedly have taken place between 1948 and 1984. In the late 1950's there has been a war between East and West in which several hundred or thousand atom bombs have been dropped. Immense destruction has been caused, and the world has fallen into the grips of three dictatorships with almost identical methods, ideologies, and material conditions. These three powers are for ever at war with one another. It is in the interest of each to remain so, for war has become a permanent feature of the politics and economy of each power. The purpose of war is no longer to destroy the enemy, since the attempt on the part of any power to win would inevitably lead to the destruction of all. However, war does enable each system to maintain its own oppression. Through war, populations may be kept in a state of almost complete poverty, subject to war measures, and agitated by propaganda. Besides giving each dictatorship complete power over its people, war is also the means of destroying that surplus wealth produced by the populations which, if the people benefited by it, might remove the conditions of oppression and ignorance necessary to the dictatorships.

The clue to Orwell's despair is contained in one sentence of Goldstein's book, in which it is explained that the principal cause for the world's division into three dictatorships was the fact that 'early in the twentieth century, human equality had become technically possible'. The positive vision of Orwell is centred in the idea of human equality, just as that of Eliot's Mr. Prufrock is in the vision of the mermaids who do not sing to him. When Orwell had to abandon the vision of human equality, he was overwhelmed by the anti-vision of a society expressly designed to perpetuate 'unfreedom and inequality'. So, too, Eliot was overwhelmed by the realization of *The Waste Land* when he discovered that the carefully sustained ironic mask of the poet satirizing the world (while he retained his own secret vision of the beauty of the past) was not an adequate attitude to the history of our time. For Orwell, the realization that freedom was decreasing all over the world after the Spanish Civil War, that the very ground on which the individual could stand was being cut away from under his feet, that the evidence on which he could base his own truth was vitiated before it reached him, and—most important of all—that the moment in the twentieth century had passed when all men could be equal (since governmental power everywhere was being concentrated into the hands of men who regarded equality 'not as an ideal to be striven after, but a danger to be averted') led directly into the despair of *1984*.

5

Orwell's realization that his vision of human equality could not be fulfilled was the result of his experiences in the Spanish Civil War and the years which followed it. He was to a remarkable extent a man who practised what he preached and lived out what he believed, and it was his experiences of life that disillusioned him in his hopes for an egalitarian socialist world. He believed, above all, in the people—the 'proles'—not just abstractly and ideologically, but out of a desire to be one of them and to share their lives. In *Down and Out in Paris and London, Homage to Catalonia*, and the essays in *Shooting an Elephant*, he describes how he was a soldier with the anarchist troops on the Catalan front, a dishwasher in Paris (where he also spent some weeks sick in the poor ward of a hospital), and out of work in London. In the course of leading a proletarian existence, the more he encountered ideologies, the more he realized that those who were responsible for them betrayed the cause of the people, usually for theoretic reasons, but ultimately just out of the love of their own power.

In an essay called 'Looking Back on the Spanish War' (from the collection *Such, Such Were the Joys*) he relates that one of the lessons he learned from Spain was that no true history of this war is likely ever to be written; for it will consist either of lies written by the Francoists, or, if Franco is deposed, the records will have been destroyed. He goes on to reflect:

> From an anti-Fascist angle, one could write a broadly truthful history of the war but it would be a partisan history unreliable on every point. Yet, after all, *some kind* of history will be written, and after those who remember the war are dead, it will be universally accepted. So for all practical purposes it will be the truth.

and:

> What is peculiar to our age is the abandonment of the idea that history *could* be truthfully written. Nazi theory indeed specifically denies that such a thing as 'the truth' exists. There is for instance no such thing as 'science'. There is only 'German science', 'Jewish science', etc. If the Leader says of such and such an event, 'It never happened'—well, it never happened. If he says two and two are five—well, two and two are five. This prospect frightens me much more than bombs.

In the same essay he goes on to ask:

> Is it perhaps childish or morbid to terrify oneself with visions of a totalitarian future? Before writing off the totalitarian world as a nightmare that cannot come true, just remember that in 1925 the world of today would have seemed a nightmare that couldn't come true. Against that shifting phantasmagoric world in which black may be white tomorrow and yesterday's weather changed by decree, there are in reality only two kinds of safeguards. One is that however much you deny the truth, the truth goes on existing, as it were behind your back. . . . The other is that so long as some parts of the world remain unconquered, the liberal tradition can be kept alive. Let Fascism, or possibly even a combination of fascisms, conquer the whole world, and those two conditions no longer exist.

And he points to changes happening between 1925 and 1945 which are no less astonishing than would be such a transformation:

> Who would have imagined twenty years ago that slavery would return to Europe? . . . Well, slavery has been restored under our noses. The forced-labour camps all over Europe and North Africa where Poles, Russians, Jews and political prisoners of every race toil at road-making or swamp-draining for their bare rations, are simple chattel slavery.

We have here the *mise-en-scène* of *1984*. There was, of course, something in Orwell's own nature which predisposed him to be fascinated by just such a nightmare. The reader of the essay *Such, Such Were the Joys*, which is an account of his childhood at Crossgates, a private school in southern England, will be struck by certain parallels between this small hell for small boys and the larger hell which Orwell envisaged as our future. Not, of course, that this affects the plausibility of *1984*. All it shows is that Orwell was predisposed by the direction of his own fantasy to perceive a condition of living nightmare.

The limits of Orwell's interest and understanding of life are as sharply defined as the quite different ones of Eliot, on which they do not converge at any point. Commenting on the changes which have taken place in education since he was at Crossgates, he coolly observes: 'Religious belief, for instance, has largely vanished,

dragging other kinds of nonsense after it.' And we are to understand that the principal tortures of Crossgates come under the
headings of: 'God, Latin, the cane, class distinctions, and sexual
taboos'. From this it is evident that Eliot's religion and traditionalism would provide no way in Orwell's mind out of the
social hell of *1984*. In fact, when he describes the 'death-wor-
shipping' religion of the inhabitants of Eurasia, we cannot help
suspecting that he is thinking of *Four Quartets*.

So that *1984* is a confined, absolute, dead-end world of despair,
like Sartre's *Huit Clos* in which there is no way out. In its different
way *The Waste Land* is just as much an enclosed universe, for it
lacks any indication that the disaster of civilization is connected
with the historic responsibility of any class or party, or that action
of any sort within history could provide a thread leading perhaps
out of a labyrinth. Eliot has put his vision of history outside any
historic time or development. Orwell lacks belief in anything
except the factual truth which 'happens behind your back' and
the vision of social equality which has become impossible. Metaphysics are not allowed to shed a ray of hope into the nightmare
of *1984*. So when Winston Smith has admitted to his torturer that
two times two do make five, even factual truth is abolished and
the doors and windows of the nightmare of a totalitarian world
are shut on mankind, presumably for ever. Perhaps there is one
faint hope which is less than a hope. This is that the proles, just
because they do not participate in the thoughts of their rulers but
continue to lead a feckless existence within the confines of their
misery, may keep certain minimal values of the human mind and
body alive. But they can do so really only because they accept
the worst and have abolished hope. Their victory is one of quiet-
ism, and is related to the situation which Orwell discusses in his
essay *Inside the Whale* on Henry Miller's *Tropic of Cancer*:

> It seems likely . . . that in the remaining years of free speech any
> novel worth reading will follow more or less along the lines that
> Miller has followed—I do not mean in technique or subject matter,
> but in implied outlook. The passive attitude will come back, and
> it will be more consciously passive than before. Progress and reac-
> tion have both turned out to be swindles. Seemingly there is
> nothing left but quietism—robbing reality of its terrors by simply

submitting to it. Get inside the whale—or rather, admit you are inside the whale (for you *are*, of course). Give yourself over to the world-process, stop fighting against it or pretending that you control it; simply accept it, endure it, record it.

Orwell's totalitarian world is one of metaphysical claustrophobia, just as Eliot, with his mind preoccupied with a condition of existence outside time, creates a world from which history offers no exit. Nevertheless, neither vision strains our credulity, partly because each is so intensely imagined, and partly because the conditions of life on our planet have altered and are altering so rapidly that the worst seems even more possible than the best. We live in an epoch without historic precedent, which may indeed be a kind of post-history, as unrelated to all we know of history as is unknown pre-history. And this world which offers two futures may offer no future. Governments which possess atomic and hydrogen bombs may interlock us in a cancelling out of opposed mechanical forces which leave human beings powerless.

Perhaps we can console ourselves by reflecting that *The Waste Land* and *1984* are the exaggerated visions of men each of whom only sees half—a different half—of living. But all the same these two halves add up to something like a whole, and we have an uneasy feeling that both *The Waste Land* and *1984* describe circumstances *which have already happened.*

One reason for suspecting this is that the consciousness of the state of civilization is not decided at all places at the same time. Something that happens hundreds of miles away may decide not only our history, but also the moral state of civilization everywhere. Thus loss of freedom on a sufficiently large scale in one area affects freedom everywhere: not only does it produce a political situation in which people in other places, feeling themselves threatened, also curtail their freedom, but the necessity of having to think about freedom actually turns men's minds away from the freest areas of living, which are those where one does not have to think about freedom but breathes it in like the air. This change of feeling is measured quickly enough in results—for example, in the arts the decline of individualist vision is one symptomatic result of it. Men are less free if they live in a society where, although there are still free institutions, it can already be said that they must accept the situation of being 'inside the whale'.

We turn then to Eliot and Orwell, because they measure losses which are invisible, impalpable, but real. And if any consolation is provided by *The Waste Land* and *1984* it is in reflecting that the very fact of their having been written offers us, after all, a last chance. For the thing that assures us that they are fictions about a state of affairs which at all events the writer and reader do not yet wholly belong to is, indeed, their having been written. These worlds of utter despair yet contain brains and nerve centres of our kind of consciousness which can record, measure, and warn against the despair and receive the warning. For total despair, if it had happened, would be a condition where nothing which represents a recording, protesting kind of consciousness—which has links with us, and through us with a different past and future —could be written.

*   *   *   *

Winston Smith, the hero of Orwell's novel, is a representative survivor from our world of hope, occupied in the business which is central to the totalitarian ideology—manufacturing despair. He sits in an office where he destroys the evidence on which any-one could construct a picture of the past detaching yesterday's discrepancies from today's official version of what happened yesterday, which might point to a different future.

His particular job is to rewrite back numbers of *The Times*. In Eurasia all publications undergo a constant process of revision and rewriting, in order that they may conform with the Party Line of the day, which often contradicts that of yester-day or a month ago. By constantly rewriting the past, the government prevents the governed from escaping out of the prison of the present. Thus truth, where it does not suit the govern-ment's orders of that day, becomes a subjective illusion.

In such a world the ultimate aim of dictatorship is not to win wars or plan the future, but simply to perpetuate the power of an élite who exist for nothing except to perpetuate their power. In one of the torture-chamber interviews which Winston Smith has with the Party Leader O'Brien, O'Brien describes the future thus:

There will be no loyalty except loyalty to the Party. There will be no love except the love of Big Brother. There will be no laughter, except the laugh of triumph over a defeated enemy. There will be no art, no literature, no science. When we are omnipotent we shall have no more need of science. There will be no distinction between beauty and ugliness. There will be no curiosity, no enjoyment of the process of life. All competing pleasures will be destroyed. But always—always there will be the intoxication of power, constantly increasing and constantly growing subtler. Always, at every moment, there will be the thrill of victory, the sensation of trampling on an enemy who is helpless. If you want a picture of the future, imagine a boot stamping on a human face—forever.

In this world the only values which Winston Smith discovers are furtively private ones. Thus his love affair with Julia, who betrays him and whom he betrays, has a quality which is the memory of a past and obliterated life. At night he calls to mind

the gesture with which she had thrown her clothes aside. With its grace and carelessness it seemed to annihilate a whole culture, a whole system of thought as though Big Brother and the Party and the Thought Police could all be swept into nothingness by a single splendid movement of the arm. . . . Winston woke up with the word Shakespeare on his lips.

Winston is also delighted to learn that Julia has slept with many Party members. Hope lies in corruption. The love affair between Julia and Winston, with its squalor which becomes an object in itself worth pursuing (since it is the protest of sensuality against the abstract horror of the Party), provides an ironic conclusion to the relationships between uninhibited lovers freed by political revolution, which forms a recurrent theme of H. G. Wells in books like *The Dream* and *A Modern Utopia*. Winston Smith and Julia are really Wellsian lovers living in a world of controlled supply and demand, fifty years after. Wells himself, at the end of his life, lived to know that his Utopian dreams ended in such a nightmare. He explored the realization in *Mind at the End of Its Tether*.

This last book, or rather essay, of Wells is incoherent, and reflects in its style and thought the physical breaking up of Wells's old age. All the same, when almost at the end of his own powers,

Wells experienced a flaring up of that vision into the present condition of humanity which gives his early scientific stories something of the imaginative heat of poetry, and which is so absent during the long middle years when he was being a respectable leader of progressive thought. In this last book he writes:

> Our universe is not merely bankrupt; there remains no dividend at all; it has not simply liquidated; it is going clean out of existence, leaving not a wrack behind. The attempt to trace a pattern of any sort is absolutely futile.

and:

> Events now follow one another in an entirely untrustworthy sequence. No one knows what tomorrow will bring forth, but no one but a modern scientific philosopher can accept this untrustworthiness fully.

and:

> In this strange new phase of existence into which our universe is passing, it becomes evident that *events no longer recur*. They go on and on to an impenetrable mystery, into a voiceless limitless darkness, against which this obstinate urgency of our dissatisfied minds may struggle. . . .

In *1984* and *Mind at the End of Its Tether* we have reached the point of complete bankruptcy of progressive thought in the face of increased scientific knowledge and totalitarian politics. It may be said that it was inevitable that materialism would end in such a bankruptcy, but as far as having any future to offer our civilization is concerned, *The Waste Land* is no less bankrupt. And the development of Eliot's work after this can hardly be said to provide such a future, for what Eliot does is to fill up a gap by abolishing the idea of time altogether and contemplating a form of existence which is outside history. He turns all time into a perpetual present, which is exactly what Big Brother does.

However, Eliot had to do something of the sort, if only in order to be able to continue writing. For the subject matter of civilization as viewed in *The Waste Land* permits of no further development. It could only continue like this for ever, with the poet juxtaposing a fragment of the past against a fragment of the present in an eternity of desert. *The Waste Land* is essentially a poem without beginning or end, and its length is chosen (it was cut down by half according to the recommendations of Ezra Pound) to produce the maximum effect of concentration.

The literature of despair is the dead end where individual vision either goes on repeating again and again the same lesson of emptiness derived from every experience, like Céline's *Voyage au Bout de la Nuit*, or it must turn back to tradition.

But for Orwell no return either to tradition or to religion is possible. If society cannot be saved, he is scarcely interested in saving himself from society, and if it is damned, then he pins hope not to his own art or soul but to the unpolitical recklessness of the 'proles'. He was a man more deeply concerned with the political future of society than with his own life or work, though he did not believe, at the end, that any political solution was possible.

The literature of despair is, though, in another sense a literature which brings us to an end of a movement, and back to realities which preceded it, for it involves the rediscovery and definition of evil. Perhaps the greatest weakness of the individualist visionaries was their weak grasp of the problem of evil. Intensely individualistic writers like Rimbaud (until *Une Saison en Enfer*) and even Rilke and Yeats, certainly Lawrence, trusted instinctively their own inner voices, or the voices, like Yeats's spirits, which dictated to them, to distinguish between good and bad. Even Eliot in his early poems puts his trust in a power of sensibility which scarcely distinguishes between moral and aesthetic sense.

But in *The Waste Land* even if evil remains intangible, we are aware that it exists. Aesthetic sensibility can no longer grant to the poet the vision of the mermaids or of 'the fancies that are curled / Around these images' which redeems ugliness with beauty. 'The empty chapel, only the wind's home' is empty because it is voided of the spirit, and its beauty does not atone for the emptiness.

In *1984* there has been a purging by Orwell of simplified political good-and-evil, parallel to Eliot's. In the end Big Brother and his Party are not bad because they are politically reactionary or even totalitarian, but because they indulge a lust for power which approaches very nearly to a lust for pure evil. And as in

Baudelaire's Paris, the highest possible good in the conditions of
1984 has become a conscious pursuit of sensuality. For where good
is impossible, the sins of the senses can be used as a moral weapon
against abstract evil. *1984* is a political novel in which politics have
been completely purged of current assumptions such as that the
Left is good and the Right bad. We are confronted with a world
in which any side can use politics as an excuse for plunging the
world in evil.

And although there is no Christ in Orwell's world, Big Brother
is really anti-Christ. He wills that the whole society shall will
nothing except his will, he demands the love of his victims, in
their lives and in the manner of their deaths. If the idea of the
equality of man is the centre of Orwell's abandoned vision, the
idea of the will of Big Brother is the centre of his anti-vision.
Thus as we read on we realize that those slogans introduced at
the beginning of the book, which at first read like crude parodies,
are literally the moral laws of a world where Evil has become the
anti-Christ's Good. LOVE IS HATE, WAR IS PEACE, AND IGNORANCE
IS STRENGTH are the basic principles of belief for the members of
the Inner Party, and Winston Smith experiences a feeling of
conversion when he is completely convinced that a lie is the truth.
He loves Big Brother.

The tragedy of Orwell's world is that man—Big Brother—
turns himself into God, but there is no God. In Eliot's world God
exists within man, but He is outside time and outside history.
Eliot's development is from the poet of exclusive sensibility who
considers his private illuminations as being outside the society in
which he moves and lives, to the profounder realization of *The
Waste Land* that the poetic mind exists within the terms of
the state of contemporary civilization. After this immersion in the
destructive element, the poet sheds his aestheticism and develops
into the religious poet always implicit in his writing. As religious
poet, he accepts the present condition of civilization, which no
longer seems relevant to the timeless plane of religious existence.
The timelessness of *The Waste Land* is the timelessness of chaos
and destruction. That of *Four Quartets* is the timelessness of eternity.

Even though the social problem seemed insoluble Orwell could
not accept a religious solution which only offered him an escape

from time. He could not abandon the religion which was truest to himself—the religion of saving man. He retained till the end of his life his anti-religious attitude which was directed against churches that have no passion for making a juster society. He distrusted as profoundly what he called the 'mysticism' of *Four Quartets* as what he called the 'hocus-pocus' of Yeats. He felt that in his later work Eliot had put behind him the problem of civilization which he grasped at in *The Waste Land*.

This raises the question whether ultimately the points of view of Eliot and Orwell are not reconcilable. Can social passion become religious, so that when the world seems a prison it can offer something to believe in outside political power which grips all populations in totalitarianism? Is there a reality of the spirit which will ultimately save society within history and within this life? Or conversely, can religion acquire the social passion which may prevent it becoming a form of death worship which serves the interests of the totalitarians? Wells and Orwell died without answering these questions, and Eliot provides an answer which would not have satisfied them. It is the question raised too by Aldous Huxley in *Brave New World*, and he also has only been able to provide an answer which seems an evasion. Koestler states the problem in *Darkness at Noon*. Essays like *The Yogi and the Commissar*, as the title indicates, are attempts to formulate the division of the minds of intellectuals into the religiously ineffective and the politically violent. In his later work with slogans like that of 'the crusader without a cross', Koestler has not been able to formulate an answer.

The same question, in a different form, confronts literature. Can the individualist vision which implied the belief that the world could be transformed by the life which the writer envisioned—can this faith in the values of living be transferred to the new orthodoxy? Or is the return to orthodoxy just a turning away of literature from life into the shadows and acceptance of death? The present phase of almost universal discouragement in creative literature is surely the result of a profound uneasiness as to the answer to these questions.

VIII

THE THEME OF POLITICAL ORTHODOXY
IN THE 'THIRTIES

THE First World War and the peace which followed were the hard winter and brilliant spring that led to a remarkable blossoming in the 1920's of the seed planted before 1914 by the tough heroes of the modernist movement.

The war had proved the reality of a world no stranger than cubism and vorticism, no less fantastic than futurism. It had justified equally the harshness of poets who sought beautiful images amid squalor, and the complete divorce from the industrialized world of those who endeavoured to make concrete some symbol or image against reality.

Out of the seed of modernism sprang the early novels of Hemingway and Fitzgerald, the satire of Evelyn Waugh and Aldous Huxley, the despair of *The Waste Land*, the exotic visual world of the early poems of the Sitwells, the 'continuous present' of Gertrude Stein, and the exciting unacademic criticism of Edmund Wilson.

The post-war decade made it possible for all these tendencies to flower, by providing the relief and the false sunshine of what was, as far as writers were concerned, a political vacuum. It is true that the League of Nations existed and excited the idealistic support of enthusiasts. But on the whole, Disarmament Conferences by the side of the Lake of Geneva (Lake Leman, which contributes a bad pun to *The Waste Land*) were left to the politicians. The lively and intelligent members of a generation who had achieved the miracle of maturing without being sent to the Western Front, and some of those, like Hemingway, who had fought and survived, felt no obligation now to support any public cause.

Revolutions had taken place in Russia and in Eastern Europe, but to the non-political intellectuals they looked like mixtures of natural disaster, apocalyptic event, and release of individualist energy. The Soviet Union meant avant-gardistes like Alexander Blok, Maiakovsky, and Essenin, and German revolution expressionists like Ernst Toller and George Kaiser. The first years of the Russian revolution produced the futurist poetry of Maiakovsky, Alexander Blok's *The Twelve* (in which twelve soldiers of the revolutionary Red Army are identified with the twelve apostles), and early Russian films like *Potemkin* and *Ten Days that Shook the World*. Thus for some years nothing in Soviet Russia appeared to contradict the delirious individualism of the West. Still less in Germany, where people with revolutionary views rushed to extremes of self-expression in their work and lives.

The characteristic literature of the 1920's combines an extreme detachment from all social and even family responsibility with an almost hysterical attachment to values of self-expression. In Hemingway's novel *The Sun Also Rises* (*Fiesta* is the English title) the behaviour of a group of Americans and English who move about Europe on their limited means, exercising their almost unlimited capacities for drinking and having love affairs, is made to have tremendous significance. Hemingway, like Turgenev in *Fathers and Sons*, draws a picture of the manners of his time, within whose apparent triviality real feelings are discerned. What is moving about Brett and her friends is their defiant search for living experience in its least intellectualized, least socially responsible forms. They insist on life without regard to consequences, because they have been sickened by the quantity of death behind them which has been demanded in the name of expected results. Their folly has something heroic about it, and the feelings which emerge from beneath a surface of sensationalism are touching. In portraying as hero of his novel the narrator who has been incapacitated from the possibility of making love by a war wound, Hemingway shows intelligence which goes deeper than intellect. His hero's predicament puts him outside the time of the rest of the characters and connects the action of the book with the background of the incapacitating war.

The best writing of the 1920's curiously combines a sense of enjoyment of the things life has to offer with an underlying sense of the futility of these things. These Hemingway and Huxley characters are cut off from history, as well as from thought and religion. They live from day to day upon their senses and their nerves. In the 1920's, as I have pointed out, people asserted the force of pleasure against the nightmare deaths of the war. This tragic hedonism expressed a kind of honourable irresponsibility. To the 1920-ish characters, their behaviour appeared as a dance of life against the background of an organized dance of death. They were players who refused to take part in official games. Sitting at bars and drinking their *pernods* they had to believe that in doing so they were more validly human than, say, the gentlemen at the Geneva conferences who were satirized so effectively in Kurt Jooss's ballet *The Green Table*. Their dance in the nightclubs and bars was alive, the ballet of the conference table was organized death. Whoever took politics seriously was capable of supporting a death-bringing cause, just as bishops blessed the war.

This could not last, and the time came when the green tables were, so to speak, turned on the *pernod*-drinkers and sun-bathers. This is what happened in the 1930's.

★   ★   ★   ★

In *Inside the Whale*, his essay on Henry Miller (which is also a survey of English literature during this century), Orwell asks, writing of some of the younger English writers in the 1930's:

> Why did these young men turn towards anything so alien as Russian Communism? Why should *writers* be attracted by a form of socialism that makes mental honesty impossible?

He goes on to answer his own question:

> The explanation really lies in something that had already made itself felt before the slump and before Hitler: middle-class unemployment.

Analysing the situation, he discovers that the English middle classes had lost faith in themselves:

Who now could take it for granted to go through life in the ordinary middle-class way, as a soldier, a clergyman, a stock-broker, an Indian civil servant, or what-not?

In short, the writers supported communism because they felt the lack of something to believe in.

Compared with most writers, Orwell was like an activist broker who really carried out deals which most of them dealt with at the end of a telephone line. Therefore his opinion of his contemporaries is always worth considering. All the same, he over-simplifies his picture of the 1930's.

It was certainly unemployment but not middle-class unemployment which drew the intellectuals to communism. Middle-class unemployment produced its own kind of ideology: the scepticism about the mission of the British Empire to which attitudes as varied as Lytton Strachey's satiric historic biographies, Forster's insistence on 'personal relations', Clive Bell's and Roger Fry's theories of pure form in painting which have no connection with anything outside painting, and the sensibilities of Virginia Woolf's heroines might all ultimately be traced. Middle-class unemployment in short produced a very subtle kind of neo-middle-class complacency.

It was, really, the spectacle of working-class unemployment which produced the communism of the young writers and intellectuals. It did so by the simple operation of a sense of guilt which established a connection between social classes previously thought of as disconnected. The young man sent to Oxford and travelling on the Continent suddenly realized that the same economic process which provided him with his independence created the dependence of the workers: it could not now even give employment to those dependents. His status, his interests, his environment, perhaps even his thought, were connected as by wires and cables under the ground with the poverty of the slums, the vacuity of the lives of youths in Welsh mining villages who passed their days lying in bed because there was neither work nor amusement for them to get up to.

In the face of what appeared to be a complete breakdown of the capitalist system, communism analysed these economic relations which were the basis of all human relations, showed what was wrong, and prescribed a radical cure—the abolition of a competitive economy and the establishment of international socialism. Orwell expresses his surprise that the young writers could accept a philosophy which so obviously dealt in lies. Perhaps the reason they did so was because the lies which they suspected in their own hearts were nearer to them than the lies told by the communists. In effect, the communists said that they diagnosed the economic disease and knew the cure. They then went on to say that whoever opposed communism did so out of self-interest, however true and plausible his reasons for doing so might appear to himself. Communists provided a schematism of simplified thinking which divided all attitudes into those which were for communist revolution and those which were against it. Assuming that the misery of the workers is the greatest evil, that unemployment can be cured by communism, and that this is known to be the case, then why does so-and-so write about skulls, cacti, shadowy lives, and spiritual consolations, they asked? The answer was (*a*) because these are the stage properties of the class of the dead to which his art belongs, and (*b*) because he wishes (consciously or unconsciously and it does not matter which) to divert attention from the class struggle. It was possible to analyse all existing attitudes in this way, and still more possible to examine and accuse one's own thoughts. Communism had not provided the young writers with a belief, but it did provide them with a bad conscience. And if it be said that the debate was crude and puerile, it should be remembered that the young writers argued with their eyes stared into by the eyes of the unemployed, to whom there were later added the eyes of the victims of the concentration camps, and all the dead of the coming war.

In the midst of a conflict in which one side analyses the causes of palpable wrongs which the other side pretends do not exist, it is easy if one is, for example, a university student, to be persuaded that scruples which deter one from taking an active part in the struggle are really the expression of secret allegiance to the side to which, by birth and interest, one belongs. All the same, it was communist distortion of 'the truth which goes on behind your back' which really did prevent many intellectuals from 'believing' in communism, even though they pleaded guilty to the communist arguments which accused them of self-interest. If the history of literary ideas in the 1930's is ever written, I am sure that what I have here written will be vindicated. For nearly all writers, communism was a matter of conscience, not of belief.

★ ★ ★ ★

Regarded as a literary phenomenon, the movement of the 1930's reflected a shift from individualist vision towards an ideological orthodoxy based on a political creed. The shift was inevitable, because the events of the 1930's, which showed the interrelatedness of class interests at the base of society, shattered the myth of a completely isolated individual—anti-bourgeois and outside everything—who was the individualist writer. For with the unemployed in the industrial cities of Europe, and with intellectuals in the concentration camps of Germany and Italy, he was no longer an outsider, unrelated to anything but his work, responsible to nothing but his artistic conscience. He was as guilty as the rest of the middle class in the eyes of the proletariat, and at the same time persecuted by the fascists on account of his supposed revolutionary sympathies. The *poète maudit* of the early part of the century was transformed into the 'intellectual' opposing fascism and supporting the Spanish Republicans of the 1930's. His curse now was to be suspected by both sides, and, still more, by himself.

The tendency towards political orthodoxy was reinforced by the impasse of *The Waste Land*, a work which to the young writers who grew up in its shadow seemed above all a declaration of the complete bankruptcy of civilization. So long as they could see contemporary Europe in the image of that poem—as a place where everything had happened and fallen into ruins and there were no sides to take because nothing could be saved—they were left only with a literary problem—of writing out of a complete detachment and on the assumption that civilization was finished with. Once though (speaking metaphorically) concentration camps began to appear in *The Waste Land*, the position was entirely altered. Their sympathies were enlisted. They were called on to take sides. At the same time the possibilities of a different kind of literature based on social hope were opened to them. Significantly the titles of the two best novels of the decade express the idea of taking sides in a human cause—*For Whom the Bell Tolls* and *L'Espoir* (Hope) by André Malraux.

The stages of development from the 1920's to the 1930's and until today are reflected in the work of W. H. Auden, whose poems have an almost chameleon-like quality of taking on the colour of the time in which they were written.

From the first poems which he published in 1927 and 1928 in volumes of Oxford undergraduate verse, Auden, who was the son of a psychologist and who at school had studied science, showed to a remarkable extent a gift for inventing clinical-seeming images, like segments or specimens chosen to illustrate the behaviour of an organism from which they were dissected. A case history seems to have been transformed into a creative process in lines like these:

> Will you turn a deaf ear
> To what they said on the shore,
> Interrogate their poises
> In their rich houses:
>
> Of stork-legged heaven-reachers
> Of the compulsory touchers
> The sensitive amusers
> And masked amazers?

As an undergraduate he studied Anglo-Saxon poetry, from which he borrowed that style which encloses his analytic specimens in a language suggesting epic vastness and icy detachment. He liked inventing cryptic phrases, and posing riddles. He fills his early poems with proper names, unknown to any readers but his friends, and private jokes:

> Tonight the many come to mind
> Sent forward in the thaw with anxious marrow
> For such might now return with a bleak face,
> An image pause half-lighted in the door,
> A greater but not fortunate in all:
> Come home deprived of an astonishing end . . .
> Morgan who took a clean death in the north
> Shouting against the wind, or cousin Dodds,
> Passed out in her chair, the snow falling.

In his early poetry Auden deliberately avoids opinions, sympathies, and emotions. It is a poetry of poetic symptoms written by one who looks at all situations with a view to extracting a phrase, a line, which he then strings into a poem. These early poems remind me of those necklaces made by Esquimaux out of the white tooth of a walrus, a couple of bones, some glass beads, and other such found trophies won in the hunt or cast up on the ice-floe.

After leaving Oxford, Auden went, in 1929, to Germany, from where almost at once more formidable observations intrude among his assortment of discovered objects. Germany in his poetry is the land of new ideas, strange morals, new architecture, and the post-war collapse. All these he now brings into his poems:

> All this time was anxiety at night,
> Shooting and barricade in street.
> Walking here late I listened to a friend
> Talking excitedly of final war
> Of proletariat against police—
> That one shot girl of nineteen through the knee
> They threw that one down concrete stair—
> Till I was angry, said I was pleased.

These lines naively state an indifference which the writer cannot keep up. Just as Eliot in his early poetry looked with ironic detachment on a world of drawing-rooms whose window-panes were licked by the London fog, only in *The Waste Land* to realize a situation in which it was impossible to remain unshattered, so Auden is unable to retain his detachment in the face of the appeal of suffering. He over-asserts his indifference in the line 'Till I was angry, said I was pleased'. But in the concluding lines of the same poem we already see him having to choose between life and death, the living and the dying, love and hatred.

> Love
> Needs death, death of the grain, our death
> Death of the old gang.

The solution is love. From now on life, death, and love are thesis, antithesis, and synthesis in a dialectic which occurs again and again in his poetry. His development has been the attempt to analyse the terms in their application to the modern human condition and to solve them by an idea of love which is always changing in his poetry.

The development from the style of his earliest poetry to the technical virtuosity and the dogmatic themes of his subsequent manner was rapid. It was a shift from detachment to opinion, and from a very bare, ascetic, original style, to a great many exercises in a variety of existing conventions. Already, in his first volume, this complete change is shown in the brilliant exercise in the manner of Tennyson's *Locksley Hall*. Here he strikes the note of exhortation:

> Drop those priggish ways forever, stop behaving like a stone:
> Throw the bath-chairs right away, and learn to leave ourselves alone

> If we really want to live, we'd better start at once to try;
> If we don't, it doesn't matter, but we'd better start to die.

This development was accelerated by his German travels and by the events of the 1930's. His immediate reaction to these events is to recommend a 'change of heart' and to identify 'love' with 'life'. Everywhere he sees people and society deny 'life' because they accept conditions which frustrate 'love'. He adapts the ideas of psychiatrists—Freud and Groddeck—in his analysis of the individual, a good deal of revolutionary theory in his view of history, and Marx in his condemnation of a doomed society. He recommends in 'love' release for the individual and revolutionary change for society. The following lines show that in his early poems 'love' is psychological therapy, the releasing the negative and the inhibited forces into life:

> Sir, no man's enemy, forgiving all
> But will its negative inversion, be prodigal:
> Send to us power and light, a sovereign touch
> Curing the intolerable neural itch,
> The exhaustion of weaning, the liar's quinsy,
> And the distortions of ingrown virginity.

It is therapy for the defective and perverted lovers of Dante's *Purgatorio*: and through their 'change of heart' the salvation of society is anticipated. Auden's England of the poetry which culminates with *The Orators* is a land divided into invalids and healers, a neurotic society and a healing revolution. In spite of 'love', the civilization lamented in *The Waste Land* is rather harshly written off like a bankrupt estate:

> After some haunted migratory years
> To disintegrate on an instant in the explosion of mania
> Or lapse forever into a classic fatigue.

The Orators, a medley of verse and poetic prose, including six exuberant Odes, reads like an attack on exhausted and defeatist English life written by a pedagogue who, between fisticuffs, sarcasms, practical jokes, and exhortations, can break into beautiful lyric poetry. The question the volume sets out to answer is 'What do you think about England, this country of ours where nobody is well?' The approximate answer is to prescribe the 'love' which frees the individual from his private depressions and society from oppressive and reactionary forces. Most of the moral, or rather the psychological, choices in *The Orators* are of this comparatively simple kind—between inhibition and its reverse. There is also awareness of things more sinister: spies, bombs, wars, revolutions, and plots, among which it is not so easy to choose. The choice, when it is made, may involve condemning those who might, without the setting of war and class war, be your friends:

> Do you think that because you have heard that on Christmas Eve
> In a quiet sector they walked about on the skyline,
> Exchanged cigarettes, both learning the words for 'I love you'
> In either language:
> You can stroll across for a smoke and a chat any evening?
> Try it and see.

Looking back at it now, I see *The Orators* as a transitional poem in which Auden is largely occupied in trying to create a myth of the conflict between new and old life, on the individual and the social level. He attempts this by dividing society into friends and enemies. At first, in the *Journal of an Airman*, he defines only psychological enemies: those who walk with 'the grandiose stunt —the melancholic stagger—the paranoid sidle', etc. But in the Odes he becomes aware that the choice is not so simple: some individuals whom one would not condemn on psychological

grounds—in fact, whom one would term friends—are nevertheless enemies, because they have joined 'the other side'.

All the same, it is difficult to take such divisions quite seriously.
There is a great deal of buffoonery which takes the edge off his
satire, and indicates that his deeper nature would tell him to love
those whom he attacks. He is amusing but not happy as a sim-
plifier. Also he is an ally who tends to deflate his supposed friends.
For example, *The Dance of Death*, a short verse play which is a
kind of farcical morality, satirizes all the attitudes of the middle
class in his time. The attack is seemingly directed from the
Marxist angle, but the action ends with Karl Marx appearing on
the stage, to announce the liquidation of the dancer (who symbolizes the bourgeoisie), while a chorus chants:

> O Mr. Marx, you've gathered
> All the material facts
> You know the economic
> Reasons for our acts,

after which Marx, looking down at the dead body of the dancer,
pronounces: 'The instruments of production have been too much
for him. He is liquidated.' This buffoonery makes Karl Marx look
like one of the Marx Brothers.

Auden soon abandoned the detachment with which he wrote his
early poetry and was in search for a belief. Everything pointed to
Marxism; yet the mockery at this stage of his development really
implies the dissatisfaction of self-mockery. He could not take his
own Marxism quite seriously. His most sustained attempt to do so
is contained in *Spain*, written during the Spanish Civil War after
his return from Republican Spain, where he had gone for a few
weeks. This poem is the outstanding example of political poetry
written in the 1930's. It is a serious attempt to conform to a political
orthodoxy, yet the poetic logic of the writer's thought brings him
to a position which he obviously finds untenable, from which he
retreated immediately, and which he has never returned to.

Spain consists of a series of reflections about the past history of
Spain, the present struggle, and the future for which the Republican forces are fighting. Expressed in those terms of thesis, antithesis, and synthesis which form the basis of many of his poems,

the thesis is the Spanish past (Yesterday) whose antithesis is the revolutionary struggle (Today), and the synthesis 'love' is the wished-for Republican victory (Tomorrow). In his invocation of Yesterday the Past, Today the Present, and Tomorrow the Future, Auden is particularly successful in creating those images which seem to sum up a whole phase of history or the characteristics of a culture:

> Yesterday all the past. The language of size
> Spreading to China along the trade-routes; the diffusion
> Of the counting-frame and the cromlech;
> Yesterday the shadow-reckoning in the sunny climates.

The antithesis of Today is contained in the repeated phrase 'But today the struggle'. The significance of this is expressed in the unreserved terms which even those who could not choose communism permitted themselves when they considered the Spanish Republican cause. Life itself, being naked, replies to the spectator of history:

> What's your proposal? To build the Just City? I will.
> I agree. Or is it the suicide pact, the romantic
> Death? Very well, I accept, for
> I am your choice, your decision: yes I am Spain.

In the next stanzas the poet explores the possibilities of Tomorrow, that Perhaps which is conditional on a Republican victory:

> Tomorrow, for the young, the poets exploding like bombs,
> The walks by the lake, the winter of perfect communion;
> Tomorrow the bicycle races
> Through the suburbs on summer evenings; but today the struggle.

Meanwhile, however, the poet has to explore Today as struggle, that is, as measures necessary in order that Tomorrow may be Victory:

> Today the inevitable increase in the chance of death;
> The conscious acceptance of guilt in the fact of murder;
> Today the expending of powers
> On the flat ephemeral pamphlet and the boring meeting.

If the poeticized logic of historic necessity seems here to have betrayed the poet into admitting the necessity of betraying his own
truth, the last stanza expresses in poetry what seems a denial of
tragic poetry:

> The stars are dead; the animals will not look:
> We are left alone with our day, and the time is short and
> > History to the defeated
> May say Alas but cannot help or pardon.

George Orwell is scathing about Auden's 'acceptance of
murder', and observes that the line in which the phrase occurs
'could only be written by a person to whom murder is at most a
word'. Here he makes a criticism of the politically leftist writing
of the 'thirties which, coming from him, is justified. One might,
though, object still more strongly to a poet saying that 'History
to the defeated / May say Alas but cannot help or pardon.' What
does much great poetry do except pardon the defeated? And in
making heroes of the defeated, from antiquity until Yeats's rebels
of the Irish Rising of 1916, does tragic poetry only say
Alas?

All the same, to criticize Auden on these lines is to forget that
despite his support of the Spanish Republic his poem is an exercise
in a logic of the imagination. *Spain* is really the working out in
imaginative terms of the effects of an attitude towards the Spanish
War with which he sympathized, but which he here treats as a
hypothesis for his poetic logic. The working out of this hypothesis leads him to conclusions which when they were arrived at
were as untenable to him as they appear to Orwell. The 'truth'
of these conclusions may be, though, precisely that they are so
worked out. The reader sees that on the basis of the hypothesis
that the historic ends justify the means murder becomes necessary,
and the one end that cannot be admitted within the context of this
history is defeat. Auden's support of the Republic did not deter
him from arriving at these conclusions or from rejecting them
afterwards.

Having explored this position, Auden himself abandoned it.
Spain was a turning point in his development. After this he wrote
little about politics.

Spain reveals the great difficulties of writing a poem which supports the attitude of one side in a contemporary struggle. The poet is forced to put his imagination at the service of interpretations of the struggle which, being in fact the ideas of propagandists, are external to his own feeling. He must also insist on victory as meaning military or revolutionary success, because a tragic interpretation of the cause would, from the point of view of those participating in it, seem defeatist.

Auden, MacNeice, Day Lewis, Spender, and the other writers who made their reputations during the 1930's were well aware of these problems, and their poetic development was largely a matter of struggling with the views of the side they were supporting. The Introduction to *The Still Centre* (which contains the poems I wrote during the Spanish Civil War) is an apologia for the fact that I felt unable to write a politically orthodox poetry:

> As I have decidedly supported one side—the Republican—in that conflict, perhaps I should explain why I do not strike a more heroic note. My reason is that a poet can only write about what is true to his own experience, not about what he would like to be true to his experience.
>
> Poetry does not state truth, it states the conditions within which something felt is true. Even while he is writing about the little portion of reality which is part of his experience, the poet may be conscious of a different reality outside.

In other words, even when the political exigencies of the side I supported seemed to me to embody a truthful cause, as a poet I could only be concerned with the smaller unheroic truths of the experience I knew. The self-defence in this Introduction is a plea that the small truth of immediate experience does not contradict the larger cause if the cause itself be true. In writing of the particulars of my felt experience, I was attempting the converse of what Auden achieved in *Spain*. For he dealt with the general hypothesis of the just historic cause and allowed the logic of his imagination to develop the particular implications in action of this cause. The approach of both of us was hypothetical: my Spanish war poems were written on the hypothesis that if the cause were just then the particular truths of experience could not hurt it, Auden's that the just cause would admit the 'necessary murder'. Both points of view were, of course, totally unacceptable to the communists, whose doctrine of necessity taught them not only that necessity justified bad means and individual suffering, but also that it was necessary to deny that it did.

The kind of orthodoxy communism requires of writers in fact makes literature impossible, because it selects or dictates inspiration, theme, and attitude, matters in which the directors of the Party Line are more informed than the writer. The propagandist point of view becomes the centre of inspiration. The writers who accepted this dictation soon found themselves unable to write. Those who did not were reaching towards another kind of orthodoxy. Out of the long internecine debate about poetry and politics of the 1930's, various possible attitudes for a poetry of a just society emerged. It is worth listing these, if only because they lead into a better understanding of orthodoxy in literature:

(1) Poetry which crystallized the ideal of a socially just world. Some of my own early poems attempt this.
(2) Poetry (like Auden's *Spain*) which treats socialist interpretation of history as the hypothesis for imagining a contemporary historic conflict. Essentially, *Spain* is dramatic, and one can imagine a poetic drama on the theme of this struggle. My own poetic drama *Trial of a Judge* is also an experiment of this kind.
(3) Poetry of action about the struggle for human freedom (Cecil Day Lewis's *The Nabara*).
(4) The poetic journal which is a commentary on public and private events, in a situation where the social struggle is felt to be intimately connected with the private life (Louis Mac-Neice's *Autumn Journal*).
(5) The poetry of those who have consciously uprooted themselves from their own environment and interests, and deliberately joined another class, making its interests their own (John Cornford, Christopher Caudwell, and other poets of the International Brigade; but the example of Orwell shows how this can boomerang on the politicians).

Any one of these attitudes permits the poet to write out of his own thought or experience, while relating it to the idea of the cause which he accepts. Communists, however, object to the first because it is idealist; and to the second because it may well be ambiguous, like *Spain*, cutting both ways; the third, fourth, and fifth would all be liable to just so much censorship as would prevent the poet from remaining true to his own experience. Caudwell, in the last chapter of his interesting book *Illusion and Reality*, defines the anti-bourgeois, disciplined channels which the imagination of the 'proletarian poet' is expected to move in, when he attacks certain poets for a separation between their art and their living. By living he meant that all their attitudes should conform to a theory of revolution and the interests of the proletariat at every point. When this has happened, the 'art' that emerges could not, he thought, go astray.

★ ★ ★ ★

The creation of works of individual vision of any but secondary importance had become impossible to any poet maturing after 1930. It had become so because no writer intelligently aware of the situation could imagine himself to be standing outside the society which produced unemployment and concentration camps. Paradoxically, individualist vision had required the ascendancy of a middle class, strong, confident, and liberal enough to allow its spiritual, if not its political, opponents to criticize its materialist values—electing themselves, as it were, to be the representatives of the imaginative life within the parliament of a materialist democracy. But in the 1930's such criticism had either become forbidden—as in Germany, Italy, and *Russia*—or the oppressed, for whom the *poètes maudits* vaguely stood, had themselves become a powerfully organized interest with a materialist philosophy. Even the surrealists felt the obligation to choose between these interested groups and were forever protesting that they belonged to 'the party of the proletariat'.

In such circumstances, with society to be saved from fascism, and a war, if possible, to be averted, these poets attempted to develop the leftist orthodoxy of a poetry which portrayed humanist ideals. They failed—but they probably had certain achievements to their credit because 'for the time being' (to borrow a title of Auden's which indicates the degree of improvization in their aims) their endeavours expressed the hope which was the most vital expression of history in the decade.

The communist theorists—who now dominate half the world —made the development of a creative social orthodoxy impossible. Apart from this, the failure of the Spanish Republic and the outbreak of war removed the impulse of the anti-fascist movement. The order of all societies now became war and Cold War. We were, as Orwell states, 'inside the whale'.

Unless writers were—as Orwell suggests—to accept this situation and write quietist literature within the shadows of centralized societies taking away more and more of their freedoms and making ever deeper incursions into their lives, they had to look for the orthodoxy of an area of life outside the increasingly powerful State. Auden shocked several of his contemporaries by leaving England for the United States in 1938. But in doing so he revealed his awareness of the ineffectiveness of the attitudes he had previously adopted, when the situation was irremediably changed. From now on his work was devoted to the definition of love in terms of Christian theology. His development was immensely aided by a maturer creed which purged his conception of love of the crudity of his earlier work, in which it was equated with uninhibited living and political change. The humanism which had always been an attractive quality in his work now underwent a kind of voluntary disciplining—so that the most quoted lines he had written since the Spanish War were dropped from the *Collected Poems* in 1944, though they had been written only as recently as 1939. They are from the poem entitled '1st September 1939':

> All I have is a voice
> To undo the folded lie,
> The romantic lie in the brain
> Of the sensual man-in-the-street
> And the lie of Authority
> Whose buildings grope the sky;
> There is no such thing as the State
> And no one exists alone;
> Hunger allows no choice
> To the citizen or the police;
> We must love one another or die.

As with Eliot, conversion tended to make Auden concentrate on the interior world of the inner man, and to adopt a negative attitude to the outer world of society. All we can really hope to do is put our inner house of the soul in order:

> Instruct us in the civil art
> Of making from the muddled heart
> A desert and a city where
> The thoughts that have to labour there
> May find locality and peace,
> And pent-up feelings their release,
> Send strength sufficient for our day,
> And point our knowledge on its way,
> O da quod jubes, Domine.

If this seems to strike a note of resignation which has replaced the hope of the 1930's, it is at least still within our world, which is better than being 'inside the whale'.

At the end of his volume delivered at the University of Virginia, and published under the title *The Enchafed Flood*, Auden sums up the phases of literature I have been discussing, and takes up an attitude to the present age:

> The characteristic of the Romantic period is that the artist, the maker himself, becomes the epic hero, the daring thinker, whose deeds he has to record. Between about 1770 and 1914 the great heroic figures are not men of action but individual geniuses. . . .
> . . . We live in a new age in which the artist neither can have such a unique importance nor believes in the Art-God enough to desire it, an age, for instance, when the necessity of dogma is once more recognized, not as the contradiction of reason and feeling but as their ground and foundation, in which the heroic image is not the nomad wanderer through the desert or over the ocean, but the less exciting figure of the builder, who renews the ruined walls of the city. Our temptations are not theirs. We are less likely to be tempted by solitude into Promethean pride: we are far more likely to become cowards in the face of the tyrant who would compel us to lie in the service of the False City. It is not madness we need to flee but prostitution. . . .

This is finely said. Like many of Auden's pronouncements, however, it seems to diagnose a situation so well that, recognizing the justice of the analysis, we are likely to accept the cure without question. But certain questions should be asked. If the artists of today are builders, whom do they build for unless the tyrants of the False City? If they accept the dogma which the heroic race of artists who preceded them rejected precisely because it did not resist (or even answer, because it could not speak) the language of the False City, what reason is there to believe that this dogma will give them greater strength of resistance today than those heroic individualists had yesterday? Perhaps a dogma may save them from prostitution, but it is difficult to see how it can enable them to build the Just City, when the walls which they are building are those of the false one, which is ruled by the tyrants.

IX

THE WORLD OF EVELYN WAUGH

THE group of Evelyn Waugh's novels from *Decline and Fall* to *Brideshead Revisited* can be read almost as one developing narrative. This is not to be explained simply by the fact that some of the characters, like Lady Metroland, Peter Pastmaster, and Basil Seal, occur in several volumes, while others, like Ambrose Silk and Anthony Blanche, have such a strong family resemblance as to seem the same person under different names. Nor is it that several of his scenes are laid either in extremely sophisticated or extremely primitive surroundings; nor even that the Evelyn Waugh of his travel books, though invisible there, is very much a felt presence in the novels.

The real reason for this unity in diversity is that the novels are all essentially concerned with the same situation: the contrast between an England still dreaming of its past greatness, whose memory is evoked by country houses and the countryside, and an England of the 1920's and early 1930's in which people lived their lives as though they were part of another, and absurd, dream. Beyond these two dreams of the old England and the Bright Young Things, there is the awakening of the will into a nightmare reality beyond which there lies yet another dream: of the renewed greatness of England.

Evelyn Waugh and many of his characters belong to a generation old enough to have passed their childhoods before the First World War, though not old enough to have fought in it. They have memories of pre-war or islanded-from-war country childhoods where hunting and the nursery are the centres of a ritual of idyllic country life. At Brideshead, visits are made to the top room, where Nanny Hawkins lives, by the members of the Marchmain

family, for whom she remains a symbol of wisdom. When Basil
Seal and his sister Barbara are alone together they lapse into
nursery conversation which is slightly sinister:

'Basil, you're up to something. I wish I knew what it was.'
Basil turned on her his innocent blue eyes, as blue as hers and as
innocent; they held no hint of mischief. 'Just war work, Babs,'
he said.
'Slimy snake.'
'I'm not.'
'Crawly spider.' They were back in the schoolroom, in the
world where once they had played pirates. 'Artful monkey,' said
Barbara, very fondly.

English upper-class childhood, on a knife-edge between incredible innocence and incredible sophistication, is amongst the deeply
felt experiences of these books. Such an upbringing has surely
never been described with more objectivity and yet with more
intensity than in the portrait of a small boy—John Last—in *A
Handful of Dust*. And the boys—especially Beste-Chetwynde—at
Llanaba Castle, where Augustus Fagan presides in *Decline and Fall*,
are sharply observed.

Waugh's feeling for class is rooted in childhoods of people
simply unaware that members of any other social class exist,
except to wait on them as nannies and grooms. Apart from Nanny
Hawkins, Captain Grimes and Paul Pennyfeather are among his
few sympathetic portraits of characters not gentlemen: and of
course Grimes is a joke, but a kindly one and therefore meant to
be more than a joke. Money plays almost as much part in these
novels as class: Waugh is as unfashionably uninhibited about the
need of it if you haven't got it, and the beauty of it if, like the
Marchmains, you have, as most contemporary novelists are about
sex. Although there is a good deal of mockery of the titled and
the rich, this is never directed from the point of view of those who
are below. It is partly satiric observation of manners directed at
the Bright Young Things of the 1920's, and partly satire directed
from above, from the past, and from beyond, against the
contemporary and the decadent.

A paragraph in *Decline and Fall* is the gauge whereby Mr. Waugh
measures England. These thoughts of Paul, although used here to

produce the irony of anticlimax, none the less express his Romanticized vision of old England:

> The temperate April sunlight fell through the budding chestnuts and revealed between their trunks green glimpses of parkland and the distant radiance of a lake. 'English spring,' thought Paul. 'In the dreaming ancestral beauty of the English country.' Surely, he thought, these great chestnuts in the sun stood for something enduring and serene in a world that had lost its reason and would so stand when the chaos and confusion were forgotten? And surely it was the spirit of William Morris that whispered to him in Margot Beste-Chetwynde's motor car about seed time and harvest, the superb succession of the seasons, the harmonious interdependence of rich and poor, of dignity, innocence, and tradition? But at a turn in the drive the cadence of his thought was abruptly transected. They had come into sight of the house.
>
> 'Golly!' said Beste-Chetwynde. 'Mamma has done herself proud this time.'
>
> The car stopped. Paul and Beste-Chetwynde got out, stretched themselves and were led across a floor of bottle-green glass into the dining room where Mrs. Beste-Chetwynde was already seated at the vulcanite table beginning her luncheon.

This has that poetic lushness which is too dense in parts of *Brideshead Revisited*, where it is introduced without irony. But it contains the main theme of these novels: the contrast between dream and nightmare, the heavily charged, idealized vision of the past with the garish present.

Evelyn Waugh is a serious comedian, but his seriousness is difficult to analyse. It does not lie in any one quality. For instance, although his novels contain many touches of satire, they do not have the deadly aim and the intellectual grasp at the roots of a subject which makes satire effective. He is best when he is satirizing the Bright Young Things or Amy Macpherson and her coreligionists, subjects in themselves ludicrous, weakest when (as in the satire on modern European states in *Scott-King's Modern Europe*) an analytic grasp of a situation is required. But if he has too high a reputation as a satirist, his mastery of the comedy of manners perhaps passes unnoticed under his extravagant fantasy. I have mentioned how clearly and vividly he portrays the small boys in *Decline and Fall*. The portraits of Miss Runcible and the

6

Bright Young People in *Vile Bodies* only *seem* exaggerated: really it is their accuracy that is astonishing. Basil Seal is surely one of the best-drawn characters in modern fiction. Like Charlus or any other great character, although completely defined within the novels where he appears, he retains that mysterious quality of unexpectedness which seems to exist in a dimension of the imagination the novelist only suggests: so that when we have closed *Black Mischief* or *Put Out More Flags* we are left wondering, and imagining, what Basil is up to now.

It is this depth of observation of manners which distinguishes Waugh from the merely funny writers, and makes his comedy *serious*. It moves from the farcical to the comic, and from the comic to the tragic upon the axis of the truth of his observation of manners. As with Chaplin, we can weep with the comedian when he is being tragic and sympathize with his pathos, because we move from mode to mode of a true character portrayed. What we can least accept, though, is the sententiousness which Waugh, like Chaplin, sometimes assumes when he is being 'serious'.

The underlying seriousness of Waugh's novels lies not in their opinionatedness but in their narration of a *search*. To read several of his novels through within a few days, as I have recently done, is to feel oneself at times in the presence of a disguised spiritual autobiography. The search is religious and preoccupies the reader all the more because it is not his characters who are involved in it, but the writer himself. Perhaps one of the things which makes Evelyn Waugh primarily a comic writer is that, with all his observation of manners and behaviour, he is unable successfully to project his own spiritual struggle into a character. He creates most successfully the kind of characters whom the writer loves but despises. When he attempts a sympathetic character like Charles Ryder or Julia in *Brideshead Revisited*, he falls into the wrong kind of absurdity. He sees people from the superior point of view of one who has always his own opinions, his own very definite conceit of himself. It is he who knows what is right and wrong and good and bad; and the moment he tries to project this knowledge into the mouth of one of his characters, the situation becomes false. It is Mr. Waugh who delivers Father Rothschild's little homily in *Vile Bodies*; who gives the lecture on what is the best brandy and what are the best glasses out of which it should be drunk in the scene in the Paris restaurant in *Brideshead Revisited*; and it is he who puts Basil Seal on the side of the angels at the end of *Put Out More Flags*. These are solemn matters, we are made to feel, too solemn for these characters, so Mr. Waugh takes over.

The search begins, as it were, from the Garden of Eden, in *Decline and Fall*. The title of this novel refers, of course, to the misadventures of Paul Pennyfeather, habitually punished for crimes committed by his betters, from the moment when he is sent down from Scone College for indecent behaviour after his debagging by Lunsden of Strathdrummond to his imprisonment in Egdon Heath Penal Settlement for participating in the White Slave Traffic—an offence in which Margot Beste-Chetwynde has involved him. But the title has also a subtler irony; for *Decline and Fall*, like the novels of Ronald Firbank, deals with a world where there is in reality no Fall, nor Sin, nor Retribution.

No crime in *Decline and Fall* 'counts', and no one suffers for his offences. His four weeks of solitary confinement 'were among the happiest in Paul's life'. Captain Grimes epitomizes his own life story in one of those confessions which immediately acquits him in the court of the Republic of Love. 'Funny thing, I can always get on all right for about six weeks, and then I land in the soup. I don't believe I was ever meant by nature to be a schoolmaster. Temperament,' said Grimes, with a faraway look in his eyes— 'that's been my trouble, and sex.'

The headmaster, Dr. Fagan, remarks of Grimes that he is guilty not so much of a crime as of a 'course of action—which I can neither understand nor excuse'. However, immediately after saying this, he arranges for Grimes to marry his daughter Flossie, 'He is not the son-in-law I should readily have chosen. I could have forgiven him his wooden leg, his slavish poverty, his moral turpitude, and his abominable features. I could even have forgiven him his incredible vocabulary, if only he had been a gentleman. . . .'

Grimes, like Paul, goes through many vicissitudes, but he always turns up. What he symbolizes is rather heavily underlined. We are told he is 'of the immortals . . . Surely he had followed in the Bacchic train of distant Arcady, and played on the reeds of

myth by forgotten streams, and taught the childish satyrs the art
of love?'

Really, though, Grimes inhabits a world of a Christian or Old
Testament myth of life before the Fall, rather than of Greek
innocence. The joke of his life is that of a 'child of nature'
playing a game against man and human institutions, and sharing
the secret of his innocence with God.

This is one of the best and oldest of the jokes of the Christian—
pre-eminently the Catholic—world. It is the joke of Rabelais and
Cervantes, and we feel it whenever we love a villain. It is pre-
eminently a Catholic joke, because Catholics, with the secrecy of
the confessional, separate more sharply than do Protestants the law
of God from that of man.

But *Decline and Fall* was written, I believe, before Evelyn
Waugh's conversion to Catholicism. And it might have been the
Bible of Agatha Runcible and the other Bright Young Things in
his second book, *Vile Bodies*.

The Bright Young Things of England in the 1920's, who are
now middle-aged, correspond to the young Americans of Hemingway's Paris. They differ from Hemingway's characters in their
brittle determination not to take themselves or anything else
seriously. Hemingway's Brett and her friends lead seriously unserious lives, drinking, making love and travelling, but prepared
at any moment to look into their cups and discover an unhappy
love or a broken heart or some other symptom of their belonging
to a 'tragic generation'. What is really so attractive and seductive
about the Bright Young Things is their refusal to be tragic. They
are genuinely frivolous, real sneerers and jeerers who raise what
is after all an important moral question: Is anything worth taking
seriously? This question should only be answered in the negative
by those who are able to treat love lightly, always maintain a
certain gaiety, and never under any circumstances show the
slightest trace of self-pity.

When Adam Fenwick-Symes gets off the boat-train, after the
Channel crossing in which Miss Runcible is so shamingly 'gone
over' by the Customs officials, he suddenly remembers that he is
engaged to be married to Nina Blount. The telephone conversation which follows ('Oh, I say, Nina, there's one thing—I don't

think I shall be able to marry you after all.' 'Oh, *Adam*, you are a bore. Why not?') sets the tone of their relationship, which is spent in Adam getting, and throwing away, the financial opportunities for marriage. When Miss Runcible crashes in the racing car, she dies in a nursing-home room, where her delirium is indistinguishable from the delirium of her life:

> She was sitting bolt upright in bed, smiling deliriously, and bowing her bandaged head to imaginary visitors.
> '*Darling*,' she said, 'how *too* divine . . . how are you? . . . and how are *you*? . . . how angelic of you all to come . . .'

The novel ends with a prophetic glimpse of Adam sitting 'on a splintered tree stump in the biggest battlefield in the history of the world'. The Garden of Eden of *Decline and Fall* has given way to the false dream of the Bright Young People from which there is the awakening into the nightmare of the Third World War.

Halfway through *Vile Bodies* a conversation takes place between Father Rothschild, the Jesuit priest (who until now has been a figure of fun), Lord Metroland, newspaper proprietor, and Mr. Outrage, the Prime Minister:

> 'Don't you think,' said Father Rothschild gently, 'that perhaps it's all in some way historical? I don't think people ever lose their faith either in religion or anything else. I know very few young people but it seems to me they are all possessed with an almost fatal hunger for permanence. . . . My private schoolmaster used to say, "If a thing's worth doing at all, it's worth doing well." My Church has taught that in different words for several centuries. But these young people have got hold of another end of the stick, and for all we know it may be the right one. They say, "If a thing's not worth doing well, it's not worth doing at all." It makes everything difficult for them.'

A little later the Prime Minister asks, 'Anyway, what do you mean by everything being "historical"?'
'Well, it's like this war that's coming.' . . .
So the Bright Young Things are perhaps justified in their refusal to take life seriously, since in the 1920's it has no serious cause to offer them. However, the refusal in Waugh goes deeper than theirs, and Catholicism has not enabled him to assume an

attitude towards modern life in which the severest criticism is based on charity and sympathetic understanding. Finally it becomes a refusal of everything except a return to the old England, a land of knights equipped with machine-guns, if not clad in shining armour. In the dedicatory letter to Randolph Churchill which precedes *Put Out More Flags*, he seems to have discovered such a grail in what he terms the 'Churchillian Renaissance'. But the concluding sentences of *Scott-King's Modern Europe* (published in 1949) seem to reflect not so much a mood of despair as a feeling that the only intelligent attitude towards the modern world is one of total rejection and insistence on complete unreality.

Scott-King, after his return from modern Europe, says to the headmaster:

> 'I think it would be very wicked indeed to do anything to fit a boy for the modern world.'
> 'It's a short-sighted view, Scott-King.'
> 'There, headmaster, with all respect, I differ from you profoundly. I think it the most long-sighted view it is possible to take.'

This is petulantly negative, because there is nothing in *Scott-King's Modern Europe* to suggest what kind of a world a boy should be equipped for. The satire is directed from a point of view which, perhaps deliberately, has no possible application to the Europe that is being satirized. And although one may sympathize with the complete rejection of modern Europe, the only alternative Evelyn Waugh seems to have to offer (a deliberate cultivation of scholarship which is known not to be worthwhile) seems trivial. Not just the life satirized but the satire itself is frivolous.

In *Black Mischief*, the macabre nightmare which underlies the lives of Waugh's characters bursts at the end into the terrifying scene when Basil Seal, at the funeral feast of the Emperor Moshu, whom he has served so egregiously, discovers that he has eaten Prudence, the daughter of the British Ambassador, who was his mistress in the capital of the Azanian Empire. Waugh adds to his more and more clearly defined nightmare of the modern world a metaphor, also to be found in T. S. Eliot and Dr. Edith Sitwell: that the decadent life of an over-civilized society falling into unreality resembles the cannibalism of savages. Dr. Edith Sitwell's *Gold Coast Customs* draws a parallel between the life of London salon society and the customs of savages. The dialogue of *Sweeney Agonistes* suggests the cannibal instincts of Eliot's modern characters.

Black Mischief is Waugh's most poetic, besides being perhaps his most amusing, book, in which the need for moralizing asides is least felt. The behaviour of the Azanian Emperor and of the British and French Embassies at his capital are managed with a satire closer and more incisive than in any other of his novels. Despite the satire, one believes in the reformist zeal of the Emperor Seth, the politics of his opponents, the intrigues of the French Ambassador and the apathy of the British, much as one believes in Stendhal's Duchy of Parma. Nor is Basil Seal's conversion into a capable administrator incredible, for given sufficiently grotesque circumstances, one can believe that he would act with a zealousness of which he is incapable in England.

Basil Seal shows exceptional energy and initiative for an Evelyn Waugh hero. John Beaver, in *A Handful of Dust*, is far more characteristic. He might be described as a kind of corrupt Candide, a colourless, rather passive young man, to whom things happen, and who is transformed by events into a cold-blooded financial, sexual, and social opportunist. Paul Pennyfeather is the most attractive of this tribe, to which Adam Fenwick-Symes also belongs (Mr. Scott-King is a particularly dim specimen). John Beaver, the son of a go-getting interior-decorating mother, is the least attractive of all Evelyn Waugh's heroes.

Mean, and a hanger-on whom everyone dislikes, he is taken up by Brenda, whose husband, Tony Last, spends all their income on keeping up his Victorian Gothic house, which Brenda detests. In his tepid way, John Beaver becomes her lover. Out of this essentially comic relationship, Mr. Waugh creates a situation close to tragedy. He does so with an admirable astringency, without sentimentalizing his main characters, who are both detestable and real. In their different ways, Beaver, Tony Last, and Brenda are all selfish and self-absorbed. What Mr. Waugh succeeds in making us realize is that despite their hardness, two of these characters— Tony and Brenda—really suffer. But the tragedy is borne by their son, John, when he is killed in a hunting accident.

Mr. Waugh shows in this novel that within a situation where people act ruthlessly and selfishly, tragedy, as it were, may be distributed over their lives, though each may be incapable of feeling its intensity. John is the most sensitive and alive person among these rather dead people. When Brenda first hears of his death, involuntarily she exclaims 'Thank God', and one feels that it is this attitude of hers which has murdered him. Mr. Waugh's novels show very well that within a heartless comedy of manners there is incipient tragedy—on this level of true observation his comedy fuses with tragedy. The ending of *A Handful of Dust*, where Tony Last is lost in the Amazonian forest and falls into the hands of an elderly Englishman, to whom he reads the novels of Dickens, and who will not release him, is an admirable excursion into what in contemporary France would be called 'the absurd'.

After *A Handful of Dust*, little is added in *Scoop* and *Put Out More Flags*. But *Brideshead Revisited* is both a recapitulation of all the between-wars material, from Oxford until 1940, and an entirely new departure. It is a revolution in Waugh's whole approach to the novel which gives one something of the shock which the introduction of the 'talkies' gave to those accustomed to the silent film. In *Brideshead Revisited* he brings his novel-writing into line with that of Graham Greene, whose principal theme is the contrast between sin and sanctitude, according to the Catholic view of life as it exists in the minds of English converts.

When a comedian turns serious, one has to ask whether his consciously serious manner really says more than the unconscious seriousness of his comedy. As a comedian, Waugh has been preoccupied with serious jokes, jokes that deal with fundamentals of life and death, jokes which put the values of a God with a sense of humour above those of human institutions. His comedy can bring us face to face with hideous realities.

His serious humour has, moreover, great diversity. There is the Before-the-Fall joke of *Decline and Fall* which makes sinners sinless and every punishment let everyone off. A development of this is the forgiven, lovable sinner joke, which fuses the spirit of comedy with that of charity: for the sharpness of his observation and his parody should not allow us to forget how much affection he shows even for his most diabolical characters. Then there is the Candid Camera joke: for the real funniness of the conversation of the Bright Young Things and of characters like Ambrose Silk is in their being photographically exact. Waugh has the gift, rare among novelists, of recording conversations and scenes from real life which seem too fantastic to be real. He does not, like Forster, create the idiom of a character so convincingly that his words seem to be the invention of his behaviour, but he can imitate very well the idiom of certain types and individuals. Lastly he has the powerful imagination which can invent situations as poetically true as the endings of *A Handful of Dust* and *Black Mischief*. His weakness—which spoils his satire—is the tendency towards crude exaggeration. For instance, in *Scott-King's Modern Europe* there is an account of the formalities necessary for leaving England at the end of the war, which is inexact without being fantastic. A satirist may caricature, but he should not simply distort facts, or—like anyone else with a grievance (satire is essentially complaint)—he loses the sympathy of his audience.

Comedy often consists in saying what—if said seriously—would seem almost unsayable. Evelyn Waugh's sympathy with characters like Basil Seal who are not merely sinners but devils is an example of this. To take Basil Seal seriously is either to condemn him (as Anthony Blanche and his set, more or less, are condemned in *Brideshead Revisited*) or to excuse him, as Basil is, in fact, excused by becoming a 'reformed' character at the end of *Put Out More Flags*. Still more unsayable are those views which when stated comically affect us as social criticism, but when stated seriously are social anachronism. There is something of anachronism about the whole situation of the very aristocratic, very rich Marchmain family in *Brideshead Revisited*. The novel contains too many scenes like this (when the narrator, Charles Ryder, arrives in Venice to visit Lord Marchmain, the father of his friend Sebastian Flyte) which read like involuntary caricature:

> Plender [Lord Marchmain's valet] led us to the waiting boat. The gondoliers wore green and white livery and silver plaques on their arms; they smiled and bowed.
> '*Palazzo. Pronto.*'
> '*Si, Signor Plender.*'
> And we floated away.

'You've been here before?'

'No.'

'I came once before—from the sea. This is the way to arrive.'

'*Ecce ci siamo, signori.*'

This is, of course, realistic dialogue and description. Yet it reads like a parody of the effect of discreet but none the less vulgar glamour which surrounds the Marquis of Marchmain and his family in the mind of Charles Ryder.

Yet in *Brideshead Revisited* Evelyn Waugh adds to his nostalgic descriptions of English life what is probably the best account of Oxford in the late 1920's. The first part of the book is spent by Charles in watching his fellow-undergraduate friend Sebastian Flyte become a drunkard. Sebastian grows distrustful of this friendship, since he comes to suspect that Charles has been taken into the confidence of Lady Marchmain, who is charming, sensitive, and insidiously domineering. The second half of the novel is concerned with Charles falling in love with Sebastian's sister Julia who is married to a brash Canadian business operator.

The purpose of the novel is to show the Catholic pattern woven through the lives of the characters. Despite their folly, failure, and disorder, their religion is capable of saving them and it gives their lives significance. As Julia explains to Charles when she is trying to break away from her own marriage (and therefore also from her faith, which forbids her to marry him):

> 'I've been punished a little for marrying Rex. You see, I can't get all that sort of thing out of my mind, quite—Death, Judgement, Heaven, Hell, Nanny Hawkins, and the Catechism. It becomes part of oneself, if they give it one early enough. And yet I wanted my child to have it. . . . Now I suppose I shall be punished for what I've just done. Perhaps that is why you and I are here together like this . . . part of a plan.'

The presence of their faith in the lives of this family, sometimes clear, sometimes obscured, is vividly felt. That the Catholic characters are imperfect, dissolute, and even—like Lord Brideshead—wooden and pompous is artistically right. All the same, since none of the characters—unless perhaps Nanny Hawkins—represents the faith burning within the pure life, it is all the more necessary that in the course of the action certain ambiguities should be cleared away and the reader should feel the plan of God as a pattern distinct from a kind of spiritual glamour mingled with a good deal of worldliness which attracts Charles Ryder to the Marchmains. The distinction between the love of God and the love of man (also the subject of Graham Greene's novel *The End of the Affair*) has to be made and made clearly. For, to start off with, there is a good deal of doubt in the reader's mind whether Charles Ryder is in love with Sebastian's family on account of their style of living, or the attractiveness of Sebastian, or the aura of their religion.

The purpose of the narrative is to make clear this distinction. The great revelation is in the scene which describes Lord Marchmain's death. To prepare the reader for the full extent of this illumination, Charles Ryder is made (this is a serious artistic flaw) more obtusely and outspokenly anti-Catholic in the latter half of the book than in the first half. To some extent this may be explained on the grounds that he wants to marry Julia and that he feels her religious conscience opposes the marriage. All the same, the explanation does not hold. If Charles really cared for Julia or had any understanding of her psychology in her position, surely the last thing he would do would be to ridicule the Catholic religion to her, and least of all at the time when her brother is dying. He has not been portrayed as that kind of blunderer in his relationship with her brother Sebastian.

The crisis of the novel is when Lord Marchmain returns to Brideshead to die, after the death of Lady Marchmain. Shortly before his death, he sends away the priest who has come to visit him with these words:

> 'Father Mackay, you have been brought here under a misapprehension. I am not *in extremis*, and I have not been a practising member of your Church for twenty-five years. Brideshead, show Father Mackay the way out.'

Lord Brideshead interprets this to mean that in the event of his being *in extremis* Lord Marchmain would not refuse the priest. 'Mumbo-jumbo is off . . . the witch-doctor has gone', comments Charles Ryder, who now behaves like the caricature of a stupidly insensitive person, to Julia. Besides being unsympathetic, he is also crudely interfering. He obtains from the family doctor the opinion that if Father Mackay, against Lord Marchmain's wishes, is brought to see him again, the shock might well prove fatal. In fact the behaviour of Charles Ryder, who is presumably meant to represent the non-Catholic attitude, is of a kind to make the non-Catholic (and perhaps also the Catholic) reader wonder why Lord Brideshead does not ask him to leave the house.

At the end, despite the wishes of Charles (who is not a member of the family), Father Mackay is brought to Lord Marchmain's death-bed. Lord Marchmain, who has fallen into a coma, recovers consciousness, and makes the sign of the cross. Charles is deeply moved and the change in his attitude is presumably a preliminary to conversion:

> 'Then I knew that the sign I had asked for was not a little thing, not a passing nod of recognition, and a phrase came back to me from my childhood of the veil of the temple being rent from top to bottom.'

This scene is affecting, and we are convinced that the attitude of Charles is changed. However, even here the absolutely clear distinction between the presence of the divine and the human is not made. There is nothing to distinguish the reaction of Charles from that of a man who has been made to realize that he has shown a stupid disrespect for another man's profoundest belief and who now feels sorry for it. And when, immediately after this, Julia explains to Charles that she cannot marry him, the distinction is still less clear. It is difficult to see how she could do so, after his behaviour of the past few days.

The real failure of *Brideshead Revisited* is not confined, however, to these concluding scenes. It really lies in the character of Charles Ryder. Within his sensibility is the meeting of the minds of his Catholic friends and the agnostic views he supposedly represents. His development should record the emergence of the pattern of the true religion from the unsatisfactory lives of the Marchmains, and also from his own agnosticism.

Charles Ryder lacks the character for such a role. Despite his rationalism, he is bigot of a rather insignificant kind. He is a painter, but considers modern art 'great bosh'. He is a snob, not only in his relations at Brideshead, but in most things. He is lacking in charity. He is incapable of remaining more than faintly interested in Sebastian after his friend has become a drunkard.

Three-quarters of the way through the book we are suddenly confronted with the *fait accompli* of Charles's marriage to a lady whom he does not love, and to whom we are first introduced when he and his wife are on board ship, leaving New York for England. On board, there is also Julia, with whom Charles starts having a love affair. The reader is expected to sympathize with Charles's dislike of his vapid and pushing wife. But the assumption that the character of a person to whom one is married is an excuse for loathing her would seem as unchristian to some readers as it seems essential to the Catholic pattern of Evelyn Waugh.

For Charles Ryder to be brought to see that Lord Marchmain received spiritual comfort from Extreme Unction does not therefore convince the reader of the transcendence of God's Catholic plan. Nor does his separation from Julia shortly after this revelation, on the grounds of her religion. After all, separation from someone he loves is only a negative decision, made less impressive by the reader's suspecting that Charles Ryder loves no one. If there were an indication that by this separation Charles recognized the duty of loving his own wife, and Julia hers of loving her husband—both of whom have been portrayed as completely unlovable—then we might be convinced of a miraculous change. The lesson of God's and Nanny Hawkins's plan might be that it is your duty to love someone to whom you are bound by solemn ties; or at least charity might demand that you see no one as completely hateful. But to Julia and Charles their marriages only have the significance of sacred obstacles which prevent their marrying one another. The 'plan' of marriage in *Brideshead Revisited* looks very like a trap sprung by God to prevent people who love one another from marrying. For it appears to be a rule of Mr. Waugh's world in this novel that the married couples detest one another. Julia and Charles hate their respective partners, and Lord Marchmain hates Lady Marchmain.

The ethics of *Brideshead Revisited* are, indeed, puzzling to the uninitiated. If you are, like Sebastian, a hopeless drunkard, God according to Lord Brideshead (who despite his wooden pomposity is an authority on these matters) particularly loves you.

The sentimental friendship between Sebastian and Charles is romanticized, and the Catholics, who are always passing judgement, have nothing against it: indeed, Cara, who, although Lord Marchmain's mistress, is devout, seems to bless it as a 'phase'. As in some of Graham Greene's novels, the one offence which brings eternal damnation is getting a divorce from someone to whom you do not want to be married in order that you may marry someone you love.

However, the lack of sense of moral proportion in *Brideshead Revisited* is probably artistic rather than religious. It comes from trying to state comic seriousness—which can accept the idea that all marriages are unhappy and yet one is not allowed to marry the person one loves—as didactic moralizing, and the absurd as sober truth. When he is seriously unserious Mr. Waugh is charitable—and that, of course, is what makes his comedy serious. He caricatures his characters without failing to observe their truth, and he condemns no one. As he admits in the prefatory letter which introduces *Put Out More Flags*, he likes Basil Seal, Ambrose Silk, and the rest, and as long as he is funny about them he can go on liking them. It is when he identifies his prejudices with a moralizing religion that qualities anachronistic and absurd in his view of life—intolerance, bigotry, and self-righteousness—work against his talent, and even tend to caricature the very ideas he is supposed to be supporting. When he is solemn, his work provides an extravagant example of faith without charity. One can understand and respect the reasons which made him abandon the personal vision of the earlier novels. Yet there was more love among the innocent savages of *Decline and Fall* and the cannibals of *Vile Bodies* than we find among the Marchmains and Charles Ryder.

X

THE NEW ORTHODOXIES

O N her deathbed Gertrude Stein is supposed to have asked:
'What is the answer?' After this she lay silent for some
minutes. Then suddenly, raising herself up in bed, she asked:
'What is the question?' Then she died.

If this story be true, Miss Stein, on her deathbed, epitomized in
these two questions the literary and aesthetic movement which
began in the 1850's with Baudelaire noting that modern civilization created nothing to justify the continuation of life. Baudelaire,
entering the universe of the Divine Comedy through the gateway
of his own damnation, attempted to find his own answer to nine-
teenth-century materialism. But today we find the satanism absurd and the flowers of evil faded. Even his insistence on being
the poet pursued by furies, the albatross mocked by the hearties,
is meretricious. Yet these histrionics do not challenge his position
as the great primal modern poet. Why? The reason lies not in the
answer but in a question: 'How can modern man, with his fallen
nature, his classic past, and his role in eternity, live a significant
spiritual life within the materialism of modern civilization?'

The reason why we can respect the satanism, the albatross, and
the yearning for damnation is because they all serve to restate the
problem—to pose the question. They remind us over and over
again that man has to translate the life of his soul into the language
of the modern city.

Today there is a reaction from the great individualist visionaries
because their systems provide inadequate answers. Rilke's angels,
for example, are unsatisfactory spiritual machines invented to
cope with material machines. We can't quite believe that above
the scene of modern life in which the genitals of money breed

more money and human values are sold at a fare, there stand these objectified projections of the poetic task, converting the currency of external things into symbols of the inner imagination. Shelley thought the poets were the unacknowledged legislators of mankind; Rilke thought that poetry was a kind of bourse or exchange in which material values were converted into spiritual ones.

He had fallen, we might say, into a variety of the Shelleyan fallacy exploded by T. S. Eliot. Yet some form of this fallacy seems inevitable if the poet thinks of himself as isolated communicator of values decaying within the substance of civilization, one who has by himself to change traditional spiritual living into modern terms, when religion has proved incapable of such convertibility. Although poetry cannot be a substitute for religion the poetic function tends to become a substitute for defective spiritual institutions.

Yet, as we have seen, the task of creating substitute spiritual institutions out of the poems of individual poets, the novels of a few extraordinary novelists, who exposed their sensibilities to the lost condition of man in their time, produces inevitably a crisis of communication. In a community brought up on the Bible there is no tremendous difficulty in interpreting its symbols, though meanings may well be clouded or dense or hard. But for a writer to assume the task of Mallarmé or Joyce or Rilke, of re-experiencing everything as though it had never been experienced before, and then expressing it not in terms with which traditions and education have made us familiar but in new ones minted out of his separate sensibility, puts a tremendous burden on both writer and reader. The only justification for such esoteric search and invention is that the accepted symbols have become so worn or misused that they cannot state the experiences of the contemporary situation. Values have to be created by the total submission of poetic sensibilities to contemporary reality or by the pursuit within subjective life of symbols which can be isolated from and defended against that reality. In the end, though, as the task of individual experiencing and creating grows, it becomes increasingly more difficult for the reader to understand the significance of the writer's symbols and language, without his having experienced the process of the writer's experiencing, and inventing his terms. Hence a vast literature explaining texts and the circumstances of each writer's life has grown up around the modern movement. This, in itself, has had the effect of turning the original invention of isolated writers into an object of academic study.

With Joyce a time came when, to all intents and purposes, he invented a new language. And the difficulty is that in making new words from their derivations in a dozen different languages, and using myths taken from the cultures of as many nations, he inevitably chose those sources according to the arbitrary principle of what struck his fancy in the course of his journeyings. He was a fanatical traditionalist working within no tradition and having to invent one of his own. His work can, to a certain extent, be explained and interpreted—several books have been written to elucidate *Finnegans Wake* and *Ulysses*—but only by scholars who train themselves in the systematized scattered erudition which was his. The understanding of Joyce really implies special schools or classes where people devote themselves to interpreting the mythology which accumulated in his mind above the plan of an exile's map of Dublin and its environs. He is in himself a culture and a country with myths and dialects derived from other ones.

So the attempt of the visionary writers to create works which were substitute spiritual institutions was justified not by these novels and poems providing answers to the gap in modern spiritual life but in their stating the questions which were not being answered, measuring, as it were, the dimensions of the gap, drawing attention to the disappearance of values. Poetry could not become a substitute for religion, but it could draw or create a picture of the blank of religion and describe the modern human experiences to which the religions no longer seemed to apply. It could create what Mallarmé called an 'absence', and the symbols of the symbolists which seemed to symbolize nothing could indicate holes in the structure of society where vast symbols which once existed within the ritual of living had disappeared. Systems as fantastic as those of Rimbaud and Yeats yet show that it is not enough to have sensibility and the imagination. It is necessary imaginatively to systematize the world of the imagination. *Les Illuminations* was no

e than *A Vision*, an apparition which would save the world,
it could state the hypothesis of modern disaster which needed
an answer as apocalyptic and on such a scale, the hypothesis of an
absolutely modern world to be saved.

★   ★   ★   ★

Nor did the modern movement attack the world in which we
live only in the works of the isolated individualists, the great
lonely geniuses who stand above the landscape, utterly devoted to
receiving impressions and translating them into the language of
inner lives. It was in a real sense a movement. That is to say, there
was an idea, widely diffused by symbolists, futurists, imagists and
later taken over by the surrealists, that the human imagination
could, through art, digest and transform every manifestation of
modern life, even (and perhaps especially) the ugliest, the
aesthetically least appetizing. It was a *tour de force* of the
spirit to humanize what was most mechanical, to desire what
was most hateful—just as Parisians loved the Eiffel Tower
because, being a purely scientific demonstration of the utmost
that could be achieved in the way of steel construction, their
hearts transformed it into a specially cherished toy. Did not
Guillaume Apollinaire turn the Western Front into his private
Eiffel Tower?

Besides the achievements of the individualist giants, there was
room within modernism for an attack on industrialized civilization by lesser writers who simply had the sense of belonging to
such a general movement. Apollinaire is essentially a cavalier who
does not pretend to be a general, a twentieth-century Don
Quixote armed with a machine-gun who charges into the terrible
No Man's Land of the Western Front as though the enemy defences were windmills, and who with his gaiety, imagination, and
his love of women makes us realize (as indeed Lawrence was to do
sometimes) that if we had the courage of our humanity, chivalry
could be thought of in terms of a modern gaiety of mind and
body.

If the greatest modernists improvised substitute-spiritual-
institutions in their immensely complex works, the lesser ones
explored the possibilities of an empirical day-to-day humanism,

measuring their spirits, minds, and bodies against all that is anti-spiritual, anti-intelligent, and mechanical in the modern world, and conquering stupidity with a light-hearted avarice for life. In the world of individualist vision there are direct links between the most responsible activities and the least responsible, between the greatest seriousness and the utmost silliness, between, let's say, James Joyce's experiments and those of Gertrude Stein. For what modernism does is assert the triumph of the modern human spirit over the machine; and at times it does this by gigantic efforts of absorbing a modern experience and improvising an almost arbitrarily invented intellectual system to enclose and penetrate at every point this material, at other times by cocking a snook or making a rude noise.

*   *   *   *

There is no use lamenting over the end of this movement. The reasons for the decline, partly political and social, also, lie partly within literature itself. As we have seen, the deeper the writers of the individual vision penetrated into contemporary reality, the greater the difficulty of communication with the reader. Several works have been written during the first half of this century which should terminate not with FINIS or THE END (which was a current conclusion, I think, in the last century) but with the warning DEAD END.

Ultimately the single uniting clause of faith of the whole movement lay in the hope that the individual could create his own values and so find his personal solution for his confrontation with the modern world. Paris or London was looked on as a bundle of images striking into his mind through his sensibility. What he must do was develop his sensibility, order these impressions, and create his own harmonious inner world. The greatest writer would be he who received and transformed the greatest number of impressions and ordered them within the special inner world of his special separate vision.

Such a concept of the task of literature is—with modifications and variations—common to all the visionary writers, the modern seers. It breaks down at three points. Firstly, as I have said, the symbols become too complex, the reader cannot follow them.

Secondly, the ordering of the impressions requires a religion or philosophy. If the writer invents his own system—as most of these writers have done—or if, like Baudelaire, he interprets in his own way the religion he was born into, there inevitably comes a time when he has to meet the criticism of already existing systems. He may have rejected current beliefs for seemingly good reasons, but all the same the beliefs he improvises for himself may be less satisfactory than the traditional ones. Thirdly, society today forces us to take sides in certain social conflicts. In the latter part of the nineteenth century and at the beginning of this, people of aesthetic sensibility could regard themselves as the only civilized individuals in a world whose values were becoming totally materialist. To the extent that they cared for values of their art which they created they opposed the society in which they lived. Some of them became ecstatic saints of the cult of art, caring so little for the contemporary world that they expected nothing whatever from it—neither remuneration nor recognition. Today, to be against the society in which one lives is to be for another kind of society. 'He who is not with us is against us' is the motto of all societies in the 1950's. Rightly so, because weakness and opposition make them need complete support. It follows, then, that the opponent of his society is not just for himself and his own vision: he is forced into the position of being a subversive, social, or political opponent. Hence we intelligently read politics into all attitudes: which means that individualist vision has become a delusion.

★ ★ ★ ★

Roughly speaking, today there are three orthodoxies which influence writing.

Over a large part of the world the dominating one is the Marxist, which regards the writer as someone whose duty is to interpret into the terms of his particular medium the supposedly beneficial and absolutely necessary decrees of a Communist society. In effect the writer is simply asked to be a propagandist. But if he is a Communist he does not think of himself as such, because he believes that the Party theoreticians have complete insight into the historic forces which have to be controlled in order to fulfil the Communist destiny of the whole society. He therefore accepts their superior truth as socialist reality, and does not believe that he has any truth of his own that should conflict with it. He asks to be 'disciplined' by a 'truth' which the Party directors know better than himself.

The very presence in the world of such an orthodoxy tends to produce its opposite, a counter-orthodoxy. One effect of totalitarianism is to make us distrust individualism, not only because the individual feels weak in the face of such a machine of organized mass activity but because dictatorship itself rests on the will of one supreme individual, and therefore reveals to us the fallacy of putting trust in the authority of an unchallenged human being. Civilized men could almost accept the idea of Rimbaud as a demigod, but when the Magus was Hitler or Stalin, they remembered that men are not divine.

The second of the new orthodoxies is so vague that perhaps it is hardly correct to call it an orthodoxy at all. However, it is an unstated criterion to which many people attempt to conform in the democracies—especially in England—and it is powerful. By orthodoxy here I simply mean conformity with the pervading presence of authority which demands the 'responsibility' of the artist. In England this authority is some governmental body like the B.B.C. or the British Council or the Arts Council which patronizes writers and artists. On the whole these authorities are rather enlightened. They do not consciously attempt to dictate to those who receive their benefits what they should think or write, they do not lay down rules. All the same, the authorities are themselves responsible to a public—they are liable to be bothered by questions in Parliament, for example—and they expect those who benefit to show a proper sense of this. Also these public authorities do have a certain taste. It might be defined best, I think, as committee taste: and, to go into the matter a little further, committee taste is a nice compromise between what is conservative and what is advanced. What is advanced might further be defined as that which was most advanced at the moment when the committee first met and which will remain advanced so long as it goes on meeting: though this may be tempered a little by the opinion of independent critics occasionally penetrating into the consultations of the committee. Thus it happens that a certain modern style in the arts in England has recently acquired the qualities of that which is academic. Here I am thinking, it is true, not so much of writing as of painting and music. Publishing remains independent, whereas the patrons of the painters and the musicians are, more and more, simply Government agencies. But it is also to some degree true of writers, since writers are only in exceptional cases supported by publishers. Whereas the Arts Council or the B.B.C. buys a painting or commissions a work of music, it employs writers who cannot live by writing their books.

In America the parallel development which has led to the second kind of orthodoxy is the employment of poets by universities. The universities—no more than the corresponding agencies in England—are not, of course, to be blamed: they are to be congratulated. They have—like the English organizations—saved the writers at the time of the collapse of private patronage and of a general crisis in publishing. Their action is only the last stage in a process which begins with politics and economics. Nevertheless, the result of the entry of the poets into the universities has been a tendency of the modern movement to become academic in American poetry just as modern art has become academic in England. It may seem at present difficult to reconcile academicism with modernism. In a few years' time I fear it will be only too easy to do so. In any case, as I have pointed out, the fact that the spirit of modern art was anti-academic does not make it, once it has been accepted, any the less a highly suitable (because highly complex) subject for academic study.

In America, though, it is in criticism, much more than in poetry, that one can point to this tendency: and the fact that a good deal of this criticism is written by poets is also revealing. Such criticism assumes that writing is an intellectual process of making a work which can then be analysed back to its elements by an intellectual process. It establishes certain works as sacred texts and then proceeds to examine, analyse, and generally probe them, looking always for myths, symbols, influences, Freudian explanations, and so on.

When certain modern critics elucidate works they presuppose the presence of such a complexity of elements to be the necessary condition of art that the criticism tends to overburden the work of

art itself. Students might be puzzled to answer the question why
it is that such critics, with their grasp of necessary conditioning
complexities, are not able to write poems better than the comparatively simple-minded poets. The shock of art is lost when it is
absorbed into such a complicated machinery of exegesis. Twenty
years ago T. S. Eliot was being denounced by dons for a drunken
bolshevik. Today he is accepted, partly because we have become
familiar with his kind of sensibility (and this is a distinct gain), but
partly also because no one who can be the object of so many
university theses could possibly be regarded as a drunken bolshevik. Yet although the words 'drunken bolshevik' were and
are inexact, sometimes I wonder whether a hundred volumes
explaining the mythology of *The Waste Land* haven't done more
to weaken the impact of that poem than calling Eliot rude names
could have done. Name-calling is a reaction which at least has a
certain immediacy, whereas to go into poetry equipped with a
contemporary critic's weapons of analysis is like going into a
Shelleyan garden of sensitive plants in an armoured car.

Rimbaud recommended throwing away the dictionaries; and
he wrote to his former school-teacher Izambard, who had
returned to teaching:

> Cher Monsieur: Vous revoilà professeur. On se doit à la Société,
> m'avez vous dites; vous faites partie des corps enseignants: vous
> roulez dans la bonne ornière. Moi aussi je suis le principe: je me
> fais cyniquement entretenir; je déterre d'anciens imbéciles du
> collège: tout ce que je puis inventer de bête, de sâle, de mauvais,
> en action et en paroles, je leur livre....

Adolescent lines, and yet to anyone who has been haunted by
the muse, and who is now a functionary, there is surely something
in them that rings in the ears like a trumpet. Yeats wrote the
following poem entitled *The Scholars*:

> Bald heads forgetful of their sins,
> Old, learned, respectable bald heads
> Edit and annotate the lines
> That young men, tossing on their beds,
> Rhymed out in Love's despair
> To flatter beauty's ignorant ear.

All shuffle there; all cough in ink;
All wear the carpet with their shoes;
All think what other people think;
All know the man their neighbour knows.
Lord, what would they say
Did their Catullus walk their way?

I have seen this poem seriously attacked by a poet who is also a critic, as a betrayal of intellectual values. But as a matter of fact it contains its own kind of seriousness, the key to which is the line 'All think what other people think'. The poem is not so much an attack on scholarship as a suggestion that intellect may go wrong if it forgets that poetry before it does anything else (and, of course, it does a good deal) springs elementally out of the passion and violence of individual life. An American edition of the poems of Dylan Thomas contains an introduction by a scholar acting as midwife to a public apparently unwilling to accept new poetry unless it is served up on a dish spiced with Freud, Jung, Kierke-gaarde, Groddeck, Folklore and Symbolism. Here is a character-istic elucidation from this essay:

> The 'meat-eating sun' is a composite figure drawn from the folk-traditions of Wales, the English poetic tradition, and the Freudian synthesis. It combines references to the Welsh festival of 'meat-eating' (*ciga*) celebrated when a bullock was slaughtered, to Hamlet's theme of death ('If the sun breeds maggots in a dead dog . . .') and to the Freudian conception of the libido, the 'hunger energy' symbolized by the sun.

Although Mr. Thomas disclaims knowledge of Welsh lore, Shakespearean lore, and Freudian lore, the writer who wrote this introduction might argue, I suppose, that he reveals these influences without knowing about them. But even supposing this were true, there is surely something misleading in writing of an unconscious process of creation as though it were an intellectual one; that is, as though Dylan Thomas consciously wove such references into his poetry, as, say, Auden or Empson might do. The critics extract from poems an intellectual content which they suppose to be there and label it as the qualities which go to make up the poem, with the result that a poet younger than Mr. Thomas, reading such criticism, might well imagine that by consciously introducing such elements into his verse he might become a Dylan Thomas. Perhaps this does not matter. What does matter is that the attitude of a whole generation of writers may be made intellectually conscious where it should not be, through the influence of such criticism. A process of increasing self-conscious purposiveness in writing gradually leads to the situation where the analytic critic is almost dictating his themes to the self-conscious poet.

I do not mean that criticism should be less lax and attentive. But I think that it should be concerned with other things than intellectual analysis, things which perhaps require more attention, as certainly they require more judgement. It should be concerned, for example, with deciding whether particular lines and phrases are good. And it should be also concerned with the poet's relationship to life. Mr. Thomas writes lines, some good and some bad. He is also a rhetorical writer: but what is his rhetoric about? The analysis of the quality of the poet's feeling for life is more significant than that of the influences that enter into his poetry, and it is also less harmful.

There is a tendency for criticism today to become interlocked in a kind of vicious mental circle with creativity. The critic labels those which are the intellectual elements supposed to enter into the poem. Poets—especially young ones—are influenced by the conscious wish to put these guaranteed substances into their poems. Thus we get a process of qualities being extracted from poems which have been written and fitted into those which are being written. A kind of synthetic poetry is produced which is difficult to distinguish from real poetry, and this further complicates the role of modern criticism.

*   *   *   *

The third new orthodoxy is religious, and Christian, for the most part either Catholic or Anglican. This third development is far the most striking in literature today. It is so for several reasons. One is that against the background of totalitarianism, many writers have turned again to Christian truths which are more authoritative and more accessible than the systems which the individualist visionaries try to work out for themselves. Christianity criticizes both the personal authority of extreme individualism which produced the personal disasters of so many poets and artists, and the public authority of dictators supposedly superhuman. It warns us that the individual who listens to his inner voice is listening only to himself and that this self is a fallen self; and of the evil of absolute power. Both these warnings are reinforced by a whole series of modern examples.

There are other reasons for the return to Christian orthodoxy. One reason is that what was best in the individualist vision of the great French writers at the turn of the century was already Catholic, even if these writers had forsaken the Church, so that those who follow after are likely to turn back to what was the starting point of Baudelaire, Verlaine, and Rimbaud. Another, and most important, reason is that the individual needs the spiritual authority of the Church to strengthen him against the increasing secular authority of the State.

Nevertheless these reasons are the results of the failures of the individualist visionaries to stand alone. And they do not answer the questions of Baudelaire, made a hundred years ago, with which I opened this inquiry:

> What, under Heaven, has this world henceforth to do? Even supposing that it continued materially to exist, would this existence be worthy of the name of the Historical Dictionary? As a new example, as fresh victims of the inexorable moral laws, we shall perish by that which we have believed to be our means of existence. . . . I appeal to every thinking man to show me what remains of Life. As for religion, I believe it useless to speak of it or to search for its relics. . . .

The question which comes after the answer that any new orthodoxy can give is whether this religion when expressed in literature answers or indeed even asks the first question: 'What has this world to do?' An answer which treats this question as irrelevant is also treating the most significant development of literature during the past hundred years as irrelevant. Baudelaire and other writers felt the greatness of the past—the Bible and classical antiquity, let us say—had almost ceased to be applicable to the present. The problem was to discover the terms within literature on which the memory of past greatness could be integrated within a consciousness of the present. And, indeed, to live in the present was, as the nineteenth century ended, more and more to recognize the necessity of sacrificing the past altogether, cutting oneself off from its roots, immersing oneself in the present or even—as in Futurism—the idea of the future.

The aim of certain writers—James Joyce, Henry James, Rilke, and Eliot—might be stated as that of opening up the past to flow over the present, by imagining the present in terms of the past and the past in terms of the present. We can only describe Joyce as a revolutionary traditionalist. He seeks not just to extend a weakening past tradition of conventions and forms into the present, but to reach back into a remote past, understand and concretize its values, and interpret them into a present situation, even if the present is made to appear sordid and lost as the result of such a comparison. He throws the past into the present like a bomb. His novel *Ulysses* is a military operation of this kind. The story of the wanderings of Odysseus is interpreted into the single day of Stephen Daedalus, Leopold and Marion Bloom. With irony and poetry, Joyce establishes a system of correspondences between his characters (Bloom: Ulysses—Marion Bloom: Penelope—Stephen Daedalus: Telemachus, etc.) in the story of Bloom's wanderings through Dublin. Whether we follow the ingenious parallels or not, we feel that there has been a confrontation of a whole imagined past with a whole imagined present. Much the same confrontation takes place in the opening of the Fire Sermon in *The Waste Land*. The theme of Lawrence is also confrontation, only of a different and more primitive culture: the past, surviving within the present, of nature, instinct, and primitive society, not the intensely imagined past of literature and myth.

What is striking in all these examples is the explosive relation of the past to the present when the writer's sense of the modern is brought into juxtaposition with the past. The rejection of orthodox Christianity in modern literature was due to the fact that these writers felt that no such confrontation of the most living past and the most materialist present took place within contemporary Christianity of the Churches. For this reason, when writers return to the Church, we have to ask whether their orthodoxy realizes such a confrontation, or whether it is a partial retreat from the present into the past. Better, wiser, profounder perhaps than much that has gone before, but perhaps also an abandonment of the problem faced by literature a hundred years ago.

★　　★　　★　　★

Our generation owes to T. S. Eliot more than to any other writer the renewal of the sense of the past. Through the considerable changes of style and thought which mark his development, one quality which has remained constant is that of re-thinking the past in terms of the present.

His concept of the past has, however, altered in the course of his development. In *Prufrock* the past is a secret Grail of isolated sensibility, the vision of the Mermaids pursued within the decadence of the contemporary mockery of traditional values.

In *The Waste Land* fragments of the present are dwarfed by their confrontation with far greater and more impressive fragments of the past, in a vision of civilization from which history has been removed like the mainspring from a clock. The living contemporary sensibility only holds on to 'These fragments I have shored against my ruins'.

In *The Hollow Men* the past belongs to 'Death's other Kingdom', while the present is 'dead land', 'cactus land'—waste and desert.

The positions of life and death are thus reversed. The dead are felt to have a reality (like the persistence of the dead in Rilke) which is more vivid than the life of the living, who are the skeleton populace of a desert. In *Sweeney Agonistes*—in some ways Mr. Eliot's most interesting dramatic experiment—the heart of the matter is contained in the dialogue between Doris and Sweeney, when Sweeney says that life is:

> Birth, and copulation, and death.
>
> DORIS:
>
> I'd be bored.
>
> SWEENEY:
>
> You'd be bored.
> Birth, and copulation, and death.
> That's all the facts when you come to brass tacks:
> Birth, and copulation, and death.
> I've been born, and once is enough.
> You don't remember, but I remember,
> Once is enough.

After a song about life on a cannibal isle (which has a significance found also in Dr. Edith Sitwell's *Gold Coast Customs* and Evelyn Waugh's *Black Mischief*), the dialogue is resumed:

DORIS:
> That's not life, that's no life
> Why I'd just as soon be dead.

SWEENEY:
> That's what life is. Just is.

DORIS:
> What's that life is?

SWEENEY:
> Life is death.

In *The Cocktail Party* the psychoanalyst Reilly, who is spiritual mentor and guide to those other characters whom he helps choose their vocations in life, patches up the marriage of Edward and Lavinia, and comments:

> To send them back: what have they to go back to?
> To the stale food mouldering in the larder,
> The stale thoughts mouldering in their minds.
> Each unable to disguise his own meanness
> From himself, because it is known to the other.
> It's not the knowledge of the mutual treachery
> But the knowledge that the other understands the motive—
> Mirror to mirror, reflecting vanity.

Ordinary life seems unduly oppressed in this play, as against the spiritual ecstasy of Celia's martyrdom. This martyrdom is, of course, the play's centre, the supreme vocation chosen by the chief character, who has renounced her love affair with Edward. In the modern world of cocktail parties and totalitarianism, the martyr is certainly the symbolic figure of our time. Not far from the psychoanalyst's office and the Chamberlayne's flat, thousands of people have been martyred, and we have come to accept their being so, almost as easily as we drink Martinis.

All the same, in this representative setting of contemporary history the martyrdom is put outside that history. Celia is not martyred as the result of any action contained within the life of the play. She is simply a *martyr by vocation*: and having decided in the course of her interview with Reilly on the nature of her calling, she goes to a place called Kinkanja, outside these cocktail-party lives, where she is crucified by the natives. It is true that she has been occupied in doing charitable work among the natives, but this makes the death no realer in terms of the action of the play, in which these natives are only invoked in order that her crucifixion at their hands may be described. Unless we are to interpret the natives as somehow symbolizing modern society (and in the context of the play they do not seem a projection of the lives of the kind of social life it represents) this crucifixion has no relation to history portrayed in the play. Celia is not a martyr in the sense that she is criticizing the world and the world criticizing her by martyrdom. She is a martyr by vocation and the natives are the midwives of her death.

This seems to indicate that Eliot's orthodoxy has not given him a view of history. He still separates life sharply into past tradition and contemporary existence, death and life, with the rider added that the dead, because they belong to or are gathered into the past, are more living than the living, who are pretty well dead. Edward and Lavinia might be described as life partially resurrected (compared with the death-in-life view of *The Hollow Men*) but still with the mould and mildew of the grave hanging to their wedding garments.

In the *Four Quartets*, by envisioning the religious pattern within life, Eliot has sustained the reality of spiritual life. Yet even here his concept of tradition is of an already completed pattern, outside life, although existing within living consciousness and behaviour. The world seems to consist of the living—who are little more than ghosts—and the spirits and achievements of the dead. In relation to the dead, the living are slightly unreal, at a disadvantage on the existential plane. One asks oneself whether to Eliot, history was ever real, or rather whether anything happened within time to create the pattern of existence which is now outside our time. Or did history happen outside history?

He is, of course, right in thinking that our true greatness lies in our traditions. But our traditions are living, not by being outside life, but according to our capacity to create them in terms of our contemporary existence. That this may be achieved requires, surely, that life should not be at such a spiritual disadvantage compared with the past and the dead. Life should be capable of meeting death on equal terms, otherwise we fall into death-worship. In the Renaissance men worshipped antiquity, but they also translated it into their architecture and their statues.

Moreover, life goes on, with all its manifestations which we cannot escape from. If we allow our spiritual lives to be captured by past manifestations, to the exclusion of present ones, then the unredeemed, ugly, and uncultivated modern world will gradually cover us over. The life of the spirit may be outside time, but change nevertheless takes place, and unless we can capture the changing appearances of things with our imaginations, then we will be ghosts living outside the world. We should imagine the past as intensely as we do the present, and we should transform the past into the material of the present.

The English writer who came nearest to understanding this was D. H. Lawrence. Lawrence saw that the view of tradition which turns us into shadows pursuing the stronger and clearer contours of another shadow-kingdom—the achievements of the dead—can only withdraw us from life into a world of interior cerebration. He realized the significance of the dead having once been alive and of the fact that they created their values out of their lives, out of living, not from a rejection of life. He saw also that what is most traditional in us is not death but precisely life. Life does, after all, offer us the possibility of choosing to live; and within our own lives, even more than within works of art, is the past: the lives of our parents and forefathers, physically and consciously and instinctively existing within our blood. The past as it exists in our physical and spiritual selves is not a separate entity, a pattern outside us, shrine, museum. It is ourselves. Tradition is nature as well as myth, religion, and art. It is also the universe outside ourselves, still almost untouched by the traces of our history and civilization. And it is the instinctive life within ourselves which, with the best or the worst will, we can do little to change.

Yet the relationship between nature, instinct, and time and place (outside the present 'cerebral' civilization), with the forms of a new society, revolutionized 'for the sake of man', remain quite undeveloped in Lawrence. He lacked patience, could not tolerate at all the ugliness of industrial towns, which had to be confronted to complete his imaginative realization of his ideas, nor could he accept, either for himself or others, the discipline and method to carry out a revolution or achieve a complete work of art. Changed life was for people who could wander looking for it, over the face of the earth.

★ ★ ★ ★

The problem which has preoccupied writers during the past hundred and fifty years has been to translate the conditions created by modern industrialized society into terms of inner spiritual being, so that certain individuals at least could 'imagine that which they know' and so gain the inner control of a creative pattern over their external environment.

Until recently this problem had been thought of as essentially one for individuals. The individual writer—a Rimbaud, Rilke, or Joyce—submitted his own sensibility to a process of perceiving external events translated into the symbols of his work, where they could be related to values of past tradition. The transformed present met the apprehended past within the isolated creative sensibility of a master, who produced from the fusion a work only fully appreciated by those who could share the processes of his sensibility.

It seemed something already that a few individuals through their developed perceptions could enter into worlds of the imagination where the isolated symbols extracted from the present met the accepted symbols of the traditional past. Aesthetic consciousness was redeemed from the time-process of a blatant and despised contemporary history. J. Alfred Prufrock, just as much as the poet of the *Four Quartets*, escaped from time on to a level of experience outside history.

This could happen because both writer and reader were living within a society which—materialist though it was—nevertheless produced, as it were, areas of vacuum between the solid material objects; spaces where ideas created by unmaterialist minds could float, without need of support and yet surrounded by protecting thermos walls.

Today this is no longer possible. The looking-glass walls of the thermos have broken down, and harsh air and slivers have rushed in, while at the same time the ground on which the Bohemian picnickers stood has been torn away from under their feet.

Although the modern world is more than ever specialized, specialized knowledge has produced certain unpleasant experiences which have entered into the consciousness of everyone. The atom bomb, for example, was an unprecedented explosion, not so much because it did a great deal of material destruction, but because it went off in the middle of everyone's head. When its tower of dust had subsided, the idea that there are people with exceptional inner experiences which, when communicated, will create enormous values for whoever wishes to isolate and devote himself to understanding them had almost vanished too. At some indefinable point of our general mental make-up, the modern human consciousness had been fused into one generally shared destruction, and a poem of the end of civilization had been written on the matter of every brain.

The individualist position having been destroyed, it would therefore seem that a future literature must be based on a more generally shared and less isolated mythology.

This, of course, is one justification of the present return to orthodox Christian ideas. Yet the new orthodox writers do little to build literature upon such a foundation of life. Eliot's poetry concentrates more on death and the dead than on life and the living and Auden seems largely concerned with describing symptomatic religious experiences which should persuade him and the instructed reader to have faith. In fact, the poets who have emerged from the individualist vision now seem occupied in trying to inject metaphysics into what still remains their isolated position. Their religion is private in the sense of concentrating on each individual's feelings about his own death, his own position in eternity, his own sins, his own inner knowledge, rather than his participation in life.

Catholic novelists like Graham Greene and Evelyn Waugh have an esotericism of class rather than thought. In books like *The End of the Affair* and *Brideshead Revisited* these writers are largely preoccupied with building an upper-class situation within which

7

the rather expensive sins of their characters are possible. One has to be well off to believe that the offence which annoys God above all others is divorce.

I do not mean that the concept of martyrdom as a spiritual vocation or the feelings of Catholics about divorce are experiences which should not be written about. What I do mean is that it would be a mistake to think that religious orthodoxy in these writers has transferred to an impersonal level the task of what Rilke called 'transformation'—translating the modern experience into the symbols of the poetic imagination.

Eliot and Graham Greene still seem closer to realities when they lapse into a despairing or nihilistic view of life than when they attempt to relate the modern world to their faiths. The part of Graham Greene's vision which communicates the greatest reality of life is his view of the general squalor of modern conditions— which has a good deal in common with Céline's *Voyage au Bout de la Nuit.*

It is when these writers depict some action in which their faith has to relate itself directly with the external reality of life that they leave one with a certain feeling of emptiness. There seems a curious insensibility about creating a character who, living in London and having decided to become a martyr, has to take a boat and go away from Europe in order to achieve this result. Czeslav Milosz, in his remarkable study of the Polish intellectuals, *The Captive Mind,* writes that the Polish writer of today who secretly looks for some revelation in the writing of the West, would have no interest in *The Cocktail Party,* though he would consider *The Waste Land* an interesting work. Nor would his distaste for what is generally considered poetry offering more hope than *The Waste Land* be the result of his indoctrination into communism. On the contrary, the Polish writers look to the West for an answer to communist ideas. But in a country which has been invaded by the Germans and Russians in 1939, where tens of thousands of people have been deported, and tens of thousands more exterminated, where the Warsaw rising at the end of the German occupation produced its thousands of martyrs, the idea of Celia booking a passage to some place where she would be crucified upside-down by the natives would seem strangely to combine delicacy with a certain insensitivity to the history we are living in.

A consideration of what the Polish intellectuals look to the West for may throw some light on the topics I have discussed. At the end of the war, the Polish intellectuals were for the most part inclined to be friendly to the communists, for several reasons. Perhaps the chief of these was that communism seemed to offer a solution of their aesthetic problems as writers. Communism made them believe that the great schism between the writer and the community (whether this be thought of as 'the people' or as the means of production) had been abolished: They thought, as Milosz records:

> Dialectical materialism has united everyone, and philosophy (i.e. dialectics) once more determines the patterns of life. It is beginning to be regarded with a respect once reserved only for a force on which important things depend: bread and milk for one's children, one's own happiness and safety. The intellectual has once more become useful. . . . He has been restored to society.

That a great many writers in the West—especially certain French ones—feel the need to be 'restored to society' does not require illustrating. Critics who utterly reject authoritarian regimes agree about this. For example, Herbert Read, in an interesting essay, *The Dereliction of the Artist*, writes that: 'The artist has gradually been excluded from the normal life of the community, in particular from the prevailing system of production.' So long as the artist was supported by an individual rich patron he could—Sir Herbert argues—produce a flourishing individualist art. But with the breakdown of such means of support and the emergence of collectivized societies, these conditions no longer hold. The argument applies to writers as well as artists.

So the Polish writers accommodated themselves to communism (though they may regret doing so now) because it seemed to reconcile the division between the writer and the community. They were to discover, though, another truth which Sir Herbert draws attention to:

> All attempts by authoritarian regimes to find a place for the artist in the modern industrial system have only turned the artist into a kind of clown, a jester whose role is to amuse the industrial worker

in his off time (decorate the canteen, etc.) or keep his mind off disturbing problems. All attempts of the State to find a place for the artist . . . have merely created a type of lifeless academicism which has no relevance to the desires and aspirations of the people at large.

The writers who now live under communism look for *something* to the West. For what? They do not quite know themselves. Milosz says that among the things they do *not* seek is to 'relinquish the feeling of responsibility for what the public gets from editors and producers. . . . The intellectual . . . makes distinctions between what is worthy of his respect in the West and what owes its success to cheap publicity appealing to the taste of a dubious "élite".'

For what, then? They look surely to the West for writers who understand that situation (already existing in the West) which tempted the Eastern writers into accepting communism; the hope that the Western writers will use their freedom to discover a resolution of the problem which is not in communist terms. Most of what they see in the West, however, is negative. For example, they look to Christianity.

> Do Western Christians take the necessary advantage of their freedom? One is forced to the conclusion that they do not. Religion has become something in the nature of a vestigial custom, instances of which one finds in the folklore of various nations. Perhaps some pressure is needed if Christianity is to be reborn. The religious fervour of the Christians in the people's democracies would seem to indicate as much. . . .

Even that which in the West appears to us to be written to oppose dictatorship, *from over there* may seem merely a confirmation of their worst fears . . . that we do not understand, that we are potential victims, that we are decadent. Or perhaps we appear to be occupied in setting up shrines—inside the belly of the whale. The Christians show little interest in the destruction of religious freedoms, being preoccupied with attaching their thoughts to a past world of the dead or a future world when we ourselves shall be dead; or with proving to themselves that they believe all the things that are most difficult to believe; or indulging in the subtleties which make them feel most sinful.

Yet the most important division of our time is between what Milosz calls the New Faith of communism based on an idea of 'historical merit and guilt', and the remnants of a Christianity 'based on a concept of individual merit and guilt'. Communism analyses the conflicts in modern society which produce poverty, crises of over-production, and war, whose symptoms are expressed in every aspect of human thought and behaviour. It offers a solution for these conflicts which consists in adapting all human activities to the social goal of communism. Control of history by the communist philosophy becomes the sole purpose of government and being governed. Everything is judged by this, what serves these ends is right, and what does not serve them, wrong. It is possible to be on the right or the wrong side of history in supporting or opposing communism, but all other moral standards are irrelevant. All the same, those who serve these ends have in approaching them judged them good. And although this is not relevant to their present and public actions, in their personal history it is an important factor, and it attaches them to a philosophy which ignores such a choice of the supposed good. It is this initial decision in favour of 'goodness' which gives communism moral force in the minds of those who are waverers, and even to some extent those who are opposed to it. Although this has nothing to do with the practice of communism, it is highly relevant to its success in the world today that very few who have chosen it have deliberately chosen evil. Communism rests on an initial, buried decision on the side of justice by those who then cease to be just, much as some Christian orthodoxy rests on the idea of Original Sin.

The Christian concept of 'individual merit and guilt' is, by its implications, the only one that has the power (a) to withstand the idea of 'historic merit and guilt', (b) to involve the individual in responsiblity for what happens to his neighbour, (c) to be the nuclear concept around which the idea of a just society, answering the communist thesis of history, might emerge. As Milosz observes:

> The Christian who rejects individual merit and guilt denies the work of Jesus, and the God he calls upon slowly transforms himself into History. If he admits that any individual merit and guilt

exist, how can he gaze indifferently at the suffering of people whose only sin was that they blocked the path of 'historical processes'?

Such a concept of Christianity holds the conscience of each accountable for the suffering inflicted by society—which happens to his neighbour. At the same time it analyses and exposes the actions of Christian apologists for communist methods, like the Dean of Canterbury, who slowly transform their God into History. Finally, through drawing attention to the responsibility of the individual who can incur merit or guilt, it puts Christian action back into history.

This, though, is exactly what the new Christian orthodox writers neglect. They are concerned with proving theology to themselves, experiencing timelessness, demonstrating the greatness of the past tradition and comparing it with the wretchedness of the present, denigrating the values of living. They evoke guilt not to prove to modern man his responsibility towards the martyrs (many of whom are liberals and Jews whom the orthodox do not always approve of), but to draw his attention to the fact that he is fallen, and to preoccupy him increasingly with his sins. None of this is finally inconsistent with the concept of the responsibility of every man to his neighbour, but in fact it serves to produce a mood of metaphysical introspection where each person examines his experience to prove that he has faith, is sinful, has a sense of timelessness, etc. The emphasis is on the inner world of isolated experience, now no longer visionary or nihilistic, but Christian, and yet still isolated from society. It is the orthodoxy of the convert preoccupied with his conversion.

Yet for writers in the West who still live in comparative freedom, and where they can receive honour for writing what they want to write, to use their freedom in order to describe death as preferable to life seems a dubious use of their position. In the first place it perhaps shows too little awareness of the fate of the millions who have experienced horrible deaths, and in the second place it fits in too well with the plans of tyrants who are only too glad to give the bourgeois the death he prefers. Of course, where there are the conditions which prevail today in so much of the world, life cannot seem attractive. All the same, if the Western writer has any responsibility it is surely to attach value to the idea of life within a pattern of society where men respect the right to exist of their neighbours.

Probably I shall be accused of writing that Christianity should become political. What I am trying to suggest is the reverse: that politics should be Christian. This, though, can only happen if the Christian accepts his responsibility within time and history. Such a responsibility would tell him that Marxism has been more successful than most philosophies in stating the problem of social justice within an industrial society, but that it has fallen into a fatal error where it disregards the rights of the individual—each separate individual—in ruthlessly supporting a supposedly just— because 'scientific'—process of history. The answer to Marxism is to accept the challenge of the necessity of worldwide social change, but at the same time to regard the individual with Christian charity and justice.